POLAR EXPOSURE

FELICITY ASTON

**WITH CONTRIBUTIONS
FROM MEMBERS OF THE WOMEN'S
EURO-ARABIAN NORTH POLE
EXPEDITION**

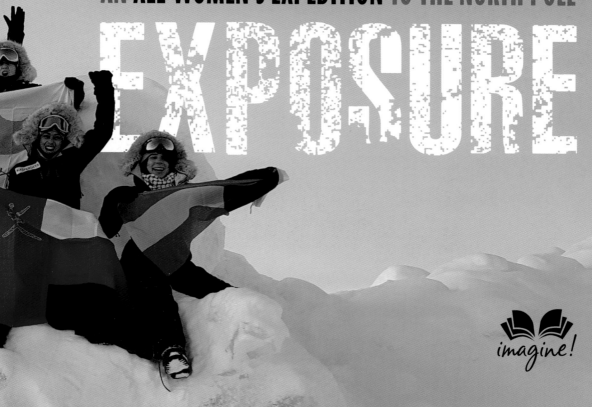

POLAR EXPOSURE

AN ALL-WOMEN'S EXPEDITION TO THE NORTH POLE

imagine!

An Imagine Book
Published by Charlesbridge
9 Galen Street
Watertown, MA 02472
(617) 926-0329
www.imaginebooks.net

Library of Congress Cataloging-in-Publication Data
Names: Aston, Felicity, author.
Title: Polar exposure : an all-women's expedition to the North Pole / Felicity Aston.
Description: Watertown: Charlesbridge Publishing, 2022. | Summary:
"The story of how British polar explorer Felicity Aston gathered a team of
ten women from across Europe and the Middle East to ski over the frozen
Arctic Ocean to the North Pole"— Provided by publisher.
Identifiers: LCCN 2021030906 (print) | LCCN 2021030907 (ebook) |
ISBN 9781623545536 (hardcover) | ISBN 9781632892447 (ebook)
Subjects: LCSH: Aston, Felicity. | Women explorers—Europe—Biography |
Women explorers—Middle East. | Skis and skiing—Arctic Ocean. | Skis and skiing—North Pole.
Classification: LCC G585.A86 A3 2022 (print) | LCC G585.A86 (ebook) |
DDC 910.911/3—dc23
LC record available at https://lccn.loc.gov/2021030906
LC ebook record available at https://lccn.loc.gov/2021030907

Display type and text type set in Agenda, Distress Compress, and Transit 521 BT
Printed by 1010 Printing International Limited in Huizhou, Guangdong, China
Production supervision by Jennifer Most Delaney
Jacket and interior design by Lilian Rosenstreich

Printed in China
(hc) 10 9 8 7 6 5 4 3 2 1

Photograph credits: All jacket, case, and interior photographs are courtesy of the following members
of the Women's Euro-Arabian North Pole Expedition: Felicity Aston, Nataša Briski, Susan Gallon,
Mariam Hameedaldin, Lamees Nijem, Misba Khan, Ida Olsson, Olga Rumyantseva, Stephanie Solomonides, and Asma Al-Thani.

Dedicated to our teenage selves—you'd be proud.

Contents

A Note on the Text

The Women's Euro-Arabian North Pole Expedition 2018 was a true collaborative effort. Eleven women from across Europe and the Middle East came together to achieve something remarkable, something that would have been impossible for any of us to have achieved as individuals. Therefore, it is fitting that an account of the expedition should follow in that same tradition of collaboration.

Polar Exposure has been written by the expedition team as a whole. Each member has contributed the best of her words, recollections, and images to create a single work. Some edits have been made to simplify or explain events, and some details have been changed for clarity, but care has been taken to remain true to the team's experiences. In presenting several different perspectives simultaneously, slight inconsistencies in accounts of the same events and chronology are inevitable. While most of these inconsistencies have been corrected, some remain in the text to reflect the reality of contradictory group memory. The result is a narrative that we hope provides new insight into the expedition experience, one in which all team members have equal voice—and equal pride.

Nervous anticipation on the helicopter taking us to the starting point of the expedition

ONE
Wake-up Call

The vibration of the helicopter shuddered through my bones, each beat heightening the sense of anticipation. It was too noisy inside the cavernous Russian workhorse to be able to communicate with my fellow passengers, even those sitting on either side of me. All we could do was look at each other. Twenty of us sat in parallel lines, military fashion, with our backs against the helicopter's shell. Silent figures puffed up in bulky down jackets and heavy ski boots, protective head gear, and superinsulated gloves the size of oven mitts. I scanned each face, faces that had become familiar over the past two years and yet remained so hard to decipher. Everyone looked drawn from lack of sleep—we had been traveling through the night—but the shadows lingering beneath the eyes had as much to do with anxiety as exhaustion. I noticed the occasional flash of a nervous smile, the fixated readjustment of a fastening, the tap of heels.

Steph caught my eye from across the cabin, fear clearly written in her expression. A Cypriot with a naturally chaotic personality, she was perhaps not an obvious choice for a ski expedition to the North Pole, and yet she was the first person I had asked to join the team. We had skied together to the South Pole nearly a decade earlier, and I hoped this new team would be as inspired as I had been by her ability to muster determined self-discipline when it mattered. Now though, I saw that the farther north we flew, the more she was wrestling with her habitual default self-doubt and insecurity, and I worried that this time they might get the better of her.

Close by, Ida stared blankly into the middle distance. As a field guide from Sweden who had spent a lot of time in the Arctic, Ida was one of the most experienced of the group, though she had never been on a ski expedition. I knew the team would instinctively look to her for reassurance, and I could already detect the weight of that responsibility reflected in her body language. Her head was pushed forward, elbows resting on her knees, hands locked together tensely.

In contrast, Mariam rested her head against the wall of the helicopter, eyes closed, comfortable. Coming from the extreme heat of Saudi Arabia, Mariam had the least experience of all of us with anything to do with the Arctic, and yet, as always, she radiated an infectious calm. Not for the first time I drew comfort from her soulful presence and felt grateful to have her with us. I noticed Lamees watching Mariam too, and I hoped that she was also drawing a similar reassurance from the composure of our teammate.

The youngest but one on the team, Lamees had so far caused me the greatest anxiety—to the extent that in exasperation I'd confronted her with my concerns just the previous evening. It wasn't that she was in any way incapable, but her deep appreciation of the moment and her surroundings, which was such a part of who she was, often seemed to take her mind off the critical job at hand. Repeatedly I'd witnessed her wandering far from the group as she sought a moment alone in the landscape—a habit that in a hazardous environment like the Arctic pack ice could compromise her safety and that of the team. She had promised to focus more, to follow instructions when it mattered, and insisted that I could trust her judgment. I didn't doubt her sincerity but remained concerned, knowing I would need to take particular care to watch out for her on the ice.

Oddly, the person who worried me least was the one with the greatest look of terror on her face. Misba, who came from the opposite end of England from me, was a mother of two grown children. Despite her nervous expression, I knew she was a person of phenomenal courage and determination, but she was also someone who seemed crushingly oblivious to her capability. I hoped this expedition would bring her greater self-belief and confidence.

Neither was I worried about Susan. She was the only one in the helicopter who managed to look excited. Taking pictures of the others, the slender Frenchwoman flashed me a smile that made it clear how joyful she was to be on her way to the Arctic Ocean. I smiled back, reminding myself how privileged we all were to be there.

Next to her was Nataša, a Slovenian journalist who was close to me in age and the only member of the team to be anywhere near my height. She had tightly cropped white-blonde hair and confidence to match. Yet the uncertainty of what we were facing had exposed a vulnerability in her. I noted an unusual strain in her features as she fussed over her clothing in the helicopter, an outlet for inner nerves.

Beside her, Anisa from Oman sat with a fixed grin that seemed a little out of place in the tense atmosphere. As an outdoor activity instructor she had a wiry physical strength that translated into an overt confidence in her abilities. It was clear that she did not expect the expedition to hold many difficulties for her, physically or mentally. I hoped she was right.

Asma was the youngest on the team but you wouldn't know it. At twenty-six, she had the wisdom and poise of someone much older. Her physique may have been diminutive, but her quiet determination was clear to anyone. As was her loyalty. Proudly displaying the national flag of Qatar, Asma was always acutely conscious of her responsibility to represent her home country and her family. Despite her having very little previous experience, I had a feeling that if just one of us was to reach the North Pole, it would almost certainly be Asma.

As I contemplated the team, I became aware of being watched myself. It was Olga, sitting opposite me. She had been the last to join the team. As a mountaineer and guide she, like Ida, had more experience than most in the group, but her late arrival to the project had left her as rather an enigma. I often felt her ice-blue eyes on me and could never quite understand what they were revealing—was it support or judgment? Or simply a need for reassurance?

Portholes studded the helicopter's fuselage and the one closest to me was open, allowing a welcome flood of coolness into the overheated cabin. There was no view, just a glare that made me wince. My eyes painfully adjusted to the white until I could make out the features of the alien landscape below. I'd previously heard the Arctic Ocean compared to a crumpled sheet of white tissue, the crazed shell of an egg, or a cracked hide of pale leather. None of those metaphors rang true as I gazed down at the seemingly endless frozen surface. It was a landscape that was instantly intimidating.

Despite more than twenty years of polar travel, this was my first proper look, eyes wide, at true high-latitude Arctic Ocean sea ice. I had previously made ski journeys on frozen lakes, rivers, and Arctic seas at lower latitudes, but that ice, constrained by land masses, had looked very different. I had also spent two months traveling back and forth across the ice of the Arctic Ocean to the North Pole aboard the most powerful ship in the world, a Russian nuclear-powered icebreaker—but we had been traveling in high summer and the sea ice had been pocked with melt pools. It was unrecognizable as the creased and folded pack ice I now observed in early spring.

Even from the safety and relative comfort of the icebreaker, the sight of the ice had prompted an instinctive uneasiness within me, a response to the power of nature on show, but now I looked on it knowing that I was about to be set down in this unmappable, unpredictable landscape of chaotic change and left adrift, surrounded by an untested

View of the frozen Arctic Ocean from the helicopter

team. Each team member was determined to overcome whatever adversity awaited us, but I was acutely aware that most of them had never done anything like this before and so had very little idea of what that reality might be. In truth, it was impossible for any of us to know how we were going to react to the challenges of the journey that lay ahead.

The helicopter sank into a sudden fog of snow, whipped by the engines as we landed with a roar. The crew opened a door and waved us out. Crouched, head bowed away from the rotors that were still slicing the air above us, I leapt out onto the ice followed by the team and our sledges—each one the size and weight of a corpse. On the ice it was -38° Celsius (-36° Fahrenheit), a temperature at least twice as cold as the inside of any home freezer. We were eighty kilometers (fifty miles) from the North Pole. The nearest solid ground was more than five hundred kilometers (three hundred miles) away over a horizon streaked with the dark reflections of distant open water. The cold took my breath away, making it hard to call out to the team as we organized ourselves into a small huddle, shielding each other and our precious equipment from the ice-filled gusts of the downdraft as the helicopter rose back into the sky.

The noise of the departing helicopter subsided and was replaced by the deafening stillness of the frozen Arctic Ocean. The quiet left a ringing in my ears, and any sound I made was deadened, as if I was moving around inside a padded room. We had landed on a wide, flat ice floe, and underfoot our boots sank ankle-deep into a layer of fine snow. I stole a glance at the stacks of ice rubble bordering the empty pan that had been our landing pad and at the horizon that lay to our north as I pulled out my handheld global positioning satellite (GPS) unit to record our location coordinates. Waiting for the device to orient itself, I squared up to the horizon, my mind skimming over the terrain ahead and reaching out toward our distant destination. The landscape was as intimidating from the ground as it had been from the air. The mini–mountain ranges of jumbled ice debris that crowded our northward view radiated serene menace. The chaos was beautiful to look at but terrifying to contemplate navigating through. I inhaled the sharp cold, choking on every other breath and thumping my chest occasionally as if to dislodge frost from my lungs. The chill began seeping through my layers of clothing and I felt my courage falter a little. Setting out over that ice would be hard work as an individual, let alone with a novice team.

Have faith, I told myself firmly. Faith in the team. Faith in the training I'd put them all through. Faith in myself to propel us all forward. My responsibility was not just to maintain my own confidence but to conserve and build theirs, too. I turned to look at the group, now sprawled across the floe, each having extracted her own sledge and skis from the jumble of kit hauled hurriedly out of the helicopter. They were unusually quiet, and I could sense the communal doubt gathering like a thickening mist. These first experiences on the ice would set the pattern for the rest of the expedition, and in many ways our success or failure would be determined right there in those first few hushed moments.

OLGA: *My joy subsided as I faced the reality before me. As we left the helicopter, the cold immediately cut through to my flesh and gnawed painfully at my bones. When we set off, my skis constantly unfastened from my boots because my frozen hands didn't have the strength to bind them tightly enough. My heavy sledge continually got stuck and overturned as I battled to pull it through the debris of boulders and irregular slabs of ice. I was soon longing to unharness my sledge and never see it again. My face mask froze and I had to ski while looking through a narrow strip of ice-fringed fabric. Like everyone else, I had not slept the previous night, and through my restricted view I began to see mirages of concrete buildings from the corners of my eyes. Fearfully, I periodically turned around to make sure the mirages were not actually there. After a while, I stopped turning around to check and instead muttered angrily to myself,* They're not real!

Despite my warm clothes and the exertion of skiing, I got colder and colder. I quickly reached a point where everything seemed

*overwhelming—the cold, the pain, the heavy sledge, the mirages—and
I began to scream inside. We had only just begun, and already the
journey was far tougher than I had ever expected. Frost formed on my
eyelashes, then changed to ice crystals that glued my eyelashes together.
I had to remove the coating of ice from my eyes in order to see, which
was tricky to do in my heavy mittens. At times I asked myself, Am I the
only one who is suffering? Looking around, my teammates all looked
cheerful, so I pretended to be cheerful too. I took off my face mask
and gazed around me. Virgin white snow. Crystal-blue ice. Everything
sparkling and glistening. Beneath all the discomfort and struggle I felt
another emotion rise within me, one recognizing that to be there in that
second was something momentous.*

We were on our way to the North Pole.

LAMEES: *The cold. I couldn't believe the cold. Despite the air being
so frigid that my breath froze, my body suddenly felt overheated. I was
so dizzy I couldn't move. I couldn't speak. I stood motionless on the sea
ice, putting all my weight on my ski poles with my head hanging down,
lifeless. I was hot, yet all my extremities were cold as stone. My stomach
hurt and I wanted to vomit.*

*Susan, my tent-mate from France, rushed toward me. "Lamees, are
you okay?"*

*I couldn't reply. I couldn't move. My head was down, my face covered
with a thin scarf and ski goggles.*

*"Lamees, are you okay?" Susan repeated, bending down to look into
my covered face.*

I heard another voice call her away.

"Hey…don't talk to Lamees. She's praying."

**Lamees in full polar gear on the sea ice of the Arctic Ocean at temperatures of
40 below**

Where did she get that idea? *I thought, still frozen in position. Why would I be praying when it's not a break? It's not even the right time for praying.*

Even with my head spinning and stomach churning, my brain tried to understand what had given my teammate the impression that I was in prayer. My body posture, standing with my head hanging down, might have been a little similar, but it was a stretch to imagine I was praying. I could hear my teammates standing close by, talking to each other. I tried to make out the words they were saying, but it was all a jumble in my head. I tried to look up but couldn't lift my neck. My eyes wouldn't focus, so I saw nothing through my goggles but a white blur. I was incapable of attracting their attention or asking for help.

Someone else rushed toward me. "Lamees, are you all right?"

Again, that same dear teammate of mine intervened. "No one should speak to Lamees. She's praying."

All three stepped away and left me standing there, hanging from my ski poles. Felicity arrived, and when I didn't respond to her, she poked me. "Lamees, your nose is very white. You might get frostbite." She took off my goggles and examined my face. Her voice was calm but I could sense her concern. "You look very pale," she said. "Are you cold?" She plucked the woolen hat from my head and threw it on the sledge. The hat was a lovely shade of purple and had been given to me by friends as a good-luck charm for the trip. "This hat isn't meant for this temperature. Where are your face mask and down jacket?"

I pointed to my sledge, still without saying a word. She rushed there, picked out the right gear, and helped me put on my insulated face mask, my goggles, and the buff that went around my neck like a circular scarf. She handed me a bag of snacks. "You need some sugar," she said in a tone that meant it wasn't a request. I robotically filled my mouth with handfuls of the sweet snacks that we had prepared in advance, spending a whole day chopping them into bite-sized pieces for easy eating. They were hard with the cold and I couldn't taste anything, but I started to feel better. Eventually Felicity seemed satisfied I was all right.

"Don't you ever wear that hat again," she scolded through puffs of condensation. I could see well enough now to notice the strain in her expression. "This is the real thing, Lamees, and any mistake could harm you. Be careful."

That was my wake-up call. We were in the Arctic. From then on I took very good care of myself and remembered the training we'd been given. Whenever I felt cold, I stopped and put on more clothes as we'd been taught. If I felt dizzy, I snacked right away and I made sure to keep moving my fingers and toes every few minutes to avoid frostbite, just as we'd been drilled. I didn't forget that first burst of cold.

I had lost focus. But those moments alerted me to what a challenge this journey was going to be. This expedition was not just about reaching the North Pole; it was also about growing and changing for the better. That was why we had been recruited. That was why we had trained.

Our mission had begun.

For Felicity, the expedition would be her fifth visit to the North Pole but the first time on skis.

TWO

Underwear

The North Pole had never been my passion. My polar attentions had always been firmly fixed southward to Antarctica. Despite joining expeditions to Greenland and the far north of Quebec as a teenager, what truly set the course of my polar career was my first job after graduating from university. At age twenty-three I was posted for a continuous period of two and a half years at Rothera Research Station, the largest of the UK's two research facilities on the Antarctic continent. I was there as a meteorologist for the purpose of monitoring climate and ozone.

This meant that Antarctica was somewhere I got to live for a while rather than just visit, but instead of satisfying my polar curiosity, the experience only expanded my fascination. On my return from Antarctica I spent years finding and creating opportunities to travel in the relatively more accessible North, putting together ski expeditions to travel across Greenland and in Siberia, gathering whatever polar experience I could. But the real prize was always a return to Antarctica.

In 2009 I got my chance. I formed an international team of women from countries such as New Zealand, Brunei Darussalam, and Jamaica, and together we skied from the coast of Antarctica to the South Pole. The following year I was back on the Southern Continent, this time on a vehicle expedition helping to forge a pioneering route from the coast of Antarctica to the South Pole via the East Antarctic Ice Sheet. Then came a two-month ski across the Antarctic landmass from the Ross Ice Shelf to the Ronne Ice Shelf by myself. It was simultaneously the most terrifying and the most wondrous of all my polar journeys, something I will always be grateful to have experienced and something I will never feel the need to repeat.

My southern bias changed the moment I set foot at the geographic North Pole for the first time. In 2015, I stepped off an icebreaker parked on a large floe at the top of the world and onto the surface of the ice. It was as stable and solid as dry land. There was no wobble, no vibration, no give under my boot. Even as we waded into melt pools of startling turquoise blue to record size and depth and salinity, the ice didn't waver. Its surface was covered not with snow but coarse ice crystals that crunched loudly as we walked. There was no crystalline reflection of the sunlight that snow cover brings, just a uniform glare that even with sunglasses seemed to make my eyes withdraw into my head.

Tasked with collecting information about surface melt pools, I moved farther from the ship, until eventually all signs of humanity were obscured from sight. I stood in that secluded quiet taking in the uninterrupted icescape around me and letting a familiar urge take hold—a desire to know this place. I began daydreaming about skiing between the lines of eroded ice rubble I had seen on the floes and heading for the horizon through a patchwork landscape of varying blues. Over time the musing began to grow and evolve, gradually solidifying into the formation of a plan.

I had seen for myself how polar expeditions can send positive and powerful messages to a wide-ranging audience in a meaningful way. Ten years earlier, the international women's team I had created to ski to the South Pole deliberately set out to challenge perceptions of what a polar explorer looks like and, specifically, to question the limitations often assumed—still—about the capability of women (assumptions frequently made by women themselves as well as by others). I regularly received messages from people who had watched, heard, or read the story of that expedition and described how they had been inspired to think differently or to take action on a long-held and long-put-off ambition that had since come to successful fruition. It was humbling and gratifying to know that something we had done was having a direct and positive impact on the lives of people we would likely never meet. Our expedition had changed perspectives and challenged prejudice. One expedition could never hope to single-handedly change the world or end gender inequality, but we had demonstrated that it could, very effectively, make a positive difference—even if only by one person at a time.

I had also witnessed how polar expeditions have the ability to get to the heart of a person very quickly. Everything we hide behind in normal life is stripped away while living in a tent in an alien landscape. The car we drive, the area we live in, our title at work, the labels in our clothes, the numbers in our bank accounts—none of that matters anymore. When far from home, feeling tired, cold, hungry, and vulnerable, all that is left is the raw person and the essence of who they are. Rather than being left disappointed or frustrated by what emerges, I have most often been left in awe by the capacity of the human spirit. At the end of a very long, difficult day, I have seen a skier give her last piece of chocolate to a teammate she noticed was having a tougher time; on other occasions I've witnessed courageous determination to continue in the most beleaguered circumstances; epic innovation in times of crisis and strokes of quiet leadership genius from those in charge of impossibly difficult situations—leaders who expected neither reward nor recognition in return.

To go through adversity with someone is to get to know them in a way that is different and perhaps more fundamental than even those they hold closest in their life. I've found that to know a person at their most vulnerable is often to know them at their most brilliant. The simplicity of expedition existence makes particularly visible what we share as human beings and demonstrates that these shared values run far deeper than any differences. This was particularly pertinent in a world that, at that time, felt like it was being riven by values taken to extremes.

I became convinced that a ski expedition to the North Pole could be used as a lens to explore cultural relationships and to instigate greater understanding across cultural divides. The divide that interested me most was between the Arabic and European worlds, particularly when it came to women. The Middle East is not a part of the world I knew, and yet it dominated so much of the international politics and current affairs that I read and heard about almost daily. I realized that I had very little idea what the perspective of a woman my age living in the Middle East might be, and I suspected I wasn't alone. I was also aware that much of the skeletal understanding I did have was sourced solely from the media, not direct experience. In return, I wondered what preconceptions and assumptions my contemporaries in a Gulf state might have about me and my values. I felt sure that by creating a team of women from across Europe and the Middle East who would share the experience of skiing across the Arctic Ocean to the North Pole, we could collectively penetrate cultural boundaries and gain insights that are otherwise hard to achieve. I firmly believe a good idea is one that will not be dismissed. And this idea refused to go away.

To set this cultural experiment in the Arctic felt fitting. It is a part of the world where the scale of the environmental change that is taking place globally is most apparent. Facing up to the consequences of climate change—as well as limiting the anthropogenic causes—is something that cannot be achieved by one region, one country, or one political affiliation alone. It will need the whole planet. For that we

The team of women assembled from across Europe and the Gulf states to ski together to the top of the world

need intercultural understanding deep enough for the human race to collaborate on issues that surpass national or regional interests. Furthering international perspectives has never been more vital.

Nevertheless, despite creating polar expeditions for most of my adult life, making the fateful leap from enthusing over a good idea to living the reality is just as difficult, daunting, and precarious as it ever was. I do not have an office full of people to help me with a new project.

There is no big organization to fall back on for support. Everything has to be created from scratch every time, and this was no exception. It was just me, a laptop, and an idea that rapidly filled my daydreams—and some nightmares, too.

Using the international women's South Pole expedition from a decade before as a loose template, I set about finding a team for this new undertaking. It was important to me that the team should be as broadly representative as possible. This was not just to challenge the stereotypes of gender, age, religion, race, physical size, or anything else, but also to make the team as engaging as possible to the greatest number of people. I wanted anyone following the experiences of my team to find at least one member who resonated with them or reflected some aspect of their own life circumstances. I wanted to make the team and the expedition as accessible as possible, to enable anyone to put themselves in our shoes and experience what we might experience in order to gain something of use from the expedition. I set up a new page on my personal website that outlined my vision for the expedition and invited any woman from any European or Arab country who felt inspired by my idea to apply to join the team. I took pains to encourage women from groups that tend to be underrepresented, such as women in their forties or fifties, as well as women who might never have done anything like the expedition before.

Spreading the word via social media to communities and networks across as many eligible countries as I could, I was soon relieved and excited to receive a steady stream of applications. I was contacted by nearly a thousand different women, almost too many applications for me to cope with on my own. The sheer number of communications I was reading made it difficult to make comparisons, even when organized into short lists or various categories. I was taken aback by the intimacy of many of the applications. Written with deep thought and care, they afforded me vivid glimpses into the lives of strangers from worlds that were completely alien to me. I felt privileged that so many women were willing to share with me their private perspectives of the world and its issues as well as their motivations for wanting to be a part of the expedition. I admired how beautifully many of the applicants articulated ideas and thoughts that can often be hard to express clearly and with which I had struggled myself. The talent and accomplishment obvious in the applications was daunting, but it was also gratifying that my idea could attract such intensity and talent. It was clear that I had tapped into a sentiment that was felt to be of real importance by many. The reaction gave the project instant momentum and transformed it into a meaningful responsibility that I had to see through, even if only for the sake of all those hundreds of women who wrote so movingly about what it meant to them.

I have never been entirely easy with the role of selector. It is impossible not to be aware that a candidate will feel an element of judgment, no matter how sensitive and transparent I try to be when making decisions. In no way do I feel qualified to judge anybody, and yet I had to build a team. I began speaking to short-listed applicants on video calls, starting with those whose application forms had resonated most strongly with me. Once I had identified one or two key team members, I searched for complementary character types that might work well together.

It is clear to me that a team is a very different thing from a group of excellent individuals. I could assemble a group of very talented women I personally thought were amazing, but if they were all of similar character—all jokers, for example, or all fastidious or all outspoken—the team would be a disaster. I needed to create a team that comprised a mix of different character traits, styles, skills, and strengths, as well as ensuring they represented a wide range of nationalities, ages, occupations, perspectives, and lifestyles. The possible permutations were maddeningly numerous, especially as the eligibility criteria I had set were deliberately broad.

Considering the logistics of putting such a large and complex team together, as well as safety, I required all applicants to be able to speak fluent English (so that the team could communicate together in one language, even when under pressure in the field), have regular and reliable internet access, and be eligible for a full passport plus any visas needed to travel. They also needed to have an adequate state of health and fitness to be able to complete a demanding polar expedition without placing themselves or others in danger, and, finally, I insisted that they were confident swimmers.

This last requirement caused the most trouble. Many of the women I spoke to could not swim, and even though they committed themselves to learning before the expedition took place, I wasn't satisfied. We were, after all, preparing to ski over a frozen ocean, and although the prospect of coming across, much less falling into, open water might be relatively low, it was a hazard that had serious consequences and was a risk we could never fully protect ourselves against. I've been purposely dunked into polar waters on repeated occasions, either for training or to take part in "polar plunges" for fun when working as a guide in the polar regions, so I'm familiar with the shock of that menacing cold. Limbs lock and become impossible to coordinate properly, jaws flap senselessly when attempting to yell or speak, and the top of your head feels like it has been caved in with an anvil. I felt strongly that to have any hope of keeping afloat in that moment of shock, swimming had to be instinctive. I worried that a recently learned skill would be lost in the paralysis of body and mind brought on by that skull-shattering cold.

As well as these basic eligibility criteria, I had five key questions for myself written on a sheet of paper next to my laptop as I prepared to speak online to potential team members: *Are they fully aware of and prepared for the considerable time and commitment the project will demand? Are they prepared to train up to required fitness? Will they be a fun tent-mate?*

Will they use the experience for a wider purpose? Do they have a realistic expectation of what they are letting themselves in for?

The questions were intended to ensure that not only did I gain enough information about each person to be able to make an educated guess on what she might add to my evolving team, but also that each might be able to make an informed decision for herself about whether the expedition was right for her. I don't think any of us can know how we will respond to, much less enjoy, an environment as alien and extreme as the Arctic Ocean until we have tried it. But I was certain that each woman knew herself much better than I could hope to know her over the course of a single interview.

As I set up my computer for each online video call, I was oddly nervous. I knew that in addition to my assessing the candidates, they would be assessing me, too. They would need to have confidence that I could pull together the expedition I was proposing and that I would be able to provide the leadership to ensure the expedition would not only succeed but succeed safely and responsibly. I expected to be under a certain amount of scrutiny. When creating expedition teams in the past, I had always met candidates in person on neutral territory, such as borrowed office spaces, hotel lobbies, or quiet cafes—places that effortlessly promoted an atmosphere of professionalism and reassurance. This time I had no option but to use video conferencing, and it felt problematically personal. I was beamed directly into a stranger's home and couldn't help but take in the details of the spare room or hallway or garden behind them, just as I was aware that they were glancing at the apartment visible over my shoulder. It was easy to be drawn into overfamiliarity, to speak as if I were talking to a friend, and it was harder to strike the right balance between encouragement and what I saw as a responsibility to make sure that no one was under any illusion about the realities of the expedition. Yet the virtual aspect of the interviews had its advantages. I spoke to women across Europe and the Arab world, in Germany and Portugal, from Iraq to

The thought of spending time in an icy tent far from home was both appealing and frightening for many who applied to be part of the expedition.

Algeria, getting glimpses of their work environment, personal spaces, or favorite coffee shops.

I noticed when speaking to women primarily based in European countries about the issue of gender equality that there was an unmistakable sense of fatigue, a frustration that despite all the discussion, awareness, and effort to advance gender parity, change was not happening as quickly or as extensively as they felt they had the right to expect. In contrast, when speaking to women from the Arab world, there was clear excitement and pride about the progress being made to safeguard the rights of women in their societies. I was left with the impression of a generation of women enjoying the thrill of riding a wave of opportunity and potential. The more women I spoke to, the more intoxicating I found this optimism and hope. Any preconceptions I might have had about women from the Arab world began to be turned on their head from the outset.

MISBA: *Skype is a wonderful innovation but does tend to diminish people. I looked at Felicity on the screen and thought how tiny she looked. I was convinced I had little chance of being selected. I wasn't sure exactly what it was that I could offer. British Muslim women, especially in my network of friends, simply didn't do this kind of thing. Also, I was a mother! I was sure that there must be hundreds of other women from all around Europe and the Middle East who would be much better qualified for the team.*

One question Felicity asked me during the interview worried me long afterward as I agonized over the reply I had given her. "Where do you see yourself in a group while skiing—at the front, in the middle, or at the back?" she asked. After a pause I had answered, "The middle." I knew I couldn't be at the front because I definitely cannot read a map, and I wouldn't want to be at the back in case I got lost. So I answered honestly (This is me, I thought to myself), but for days I worried that my answer had shown me to be weak. I also worried that I hadn't mentioned I couldn't swim. The interview had gone so poorly that I doubted it would matter anyway. I was unlikely to be offered a place on the team.

"Welcome aboard. You're going to the North Pole!" said Felicity's email. I am not exaggerating when I say that it was an utter shock. There must be a phrase to describe the remarkable feeling of lacking confidence but succeeding anyway. Yet it was a fragile emotion, and the doubts crept in immediately. I hadn't told anyone except my daughter about the application and I wondered what my family would think, as well as work colleagues and friends from a British hiking organization I belonged to called the Ramblers.

For the wider Muslim community I knew I was going to be breaking some stereotypes and that others might need some time to get used to the idea. Although my daughter's generation was encouraged to pursue their interests, many in the community felt that women like me should be at home safeguarding our culture and religion. As I saw it, if it was all right for my children, why was it not all right for me? I wanted to show that breaking those barriers didn't mean losing my religion or culture; it was about sharing those things I care about so deeply.

When I first started joining the Ramblers on regular walks, I faced logistical challenges at home. It took the help of the children and my husband to make sure everything got done on the weekends so I could have time for the walks. We'd needed to work as a team, and I was proud of us. So when it came to telling the family about the North Pole I started with my husband. For a moment he was completely silent, and then he said, "It's extremely dangerous. Isn't it enough, what you're already doing?" When I explained why I wanted to do it, how I still wanted to grow and push myself, he was completely supportive and became my biggest source of encouragement in the months to come.

Next, I told my friends. Every week I meet up with a particular group of friends, and we host each other at our various houses in turn. When it was my turn to host, I told them I had some news to share. While serving up tea and cakes I told them I was going to the North Pole. I won't forget the look of shock on their faces as I read out the details of the expedition. But the shock was quickly followed by laughter and smiles, and without exception everyone was utterly delighted for me and completely supportive.

My friends were in awe of me, but as I learned more about the Arctic, my fears grew. I had once trekked to the summit of a mountain in Morocco on a guided expedition and experienced temperatures of -20°C (-4°F), but the North Pole, I learned, could be more than twice that cold. It was impossible to imagine such extreme conditions. The coldest it's ever been in my home city of Manchester, in what's known as the "north" of the UK (although in reality it is barely halfway up the British Isles), is when it fell to -17.6°C (0°F) in 2010. It brought the whole city—schools, factories, roads, and railways—to a complete standstill.

My impression of the Arctic, I realized, was colored by television images of polar bears stalking seals to feed their cute cubs. The North Pole we were likely to experience would be nothing like that. The polar bears—far from cute distractions—would see us as dinner and were a very real threat. The Arctic wasn't even a continent, I discovered, but a sea filled with chunks of shifting ice, which could open up and pitch the unwary into deadly cold water. The thought propelled me into learning to swim as a matter of urgency. I wanted to be good enough that by the time anyone discovered I hadn't had the skill when I applied for the expedition, it would no longer matter.

I began by watching instructional videos on the internet and then putting what I had seen into practice at the local swimming pool. At first I held on to the side of the pool, trying to push myself a little farther every time I went. Eventually I was going so frequently that I attracted the attention of the lifeguards, who were really supportive once they knew of my mission to swim and helped me with both advice and encouragement. After a while I was able to swim a hundred yards—two laps of the pool—and really enjoy the experience. I continued to go every week and joined a swimming class to build up my abilities. The success gave me the confidence that I could learn whatever skills I lacked for the expedition, but I remained nervous. I knew I would have to prove myself to a group of complete strangers.

SUSAN: *As a marine biologist I have been fortunate in my career to study marine mammals all over the world, including several places in Antarctica. Traveling from my native France to these remote and rare locations during the austral summer I came to appreciate not just the wildlife but also the beauty of this most untamed of wildernesses. I* *loved everything about it—the extreme weather, the extreme landscape, even the roughness of the seas.*

The power of nature was evident everywhere, but so was its fragility. I witnessed the effects of climate change: the retreat of glaciers, the absence of snow and ice where previously it had been copious, steadily rising summer temperatures. There is no doubt that we were witnessing global—and anthropogenic—climate change, but you don't need to travel to the ends of the earth to know that.

Global warming is impacting everyone, no matter where you are in the world. In the Arctic the changes are perhaps even more stark. Arctic sea ice is melting into the ocean and leaving behind only memories of what once was. Contrary to the Antarctic, which is rock covered by ice that is mostly mapped, the Arctic is a constantly shifting landscape of floating ice and water. Unmappable.

For me, the Arctic Ocean and the North Pole were symbols of the rapid changes affecting our entire planet. As I applied for the expedition I was deeply aware that this mesmerizing part of our global ecosystem was disappearing fast and forever. I felt I needed to see this precious part of the cryosphere, to stand on my own feet on that drifting ice at the top of the world, as a witness before it no longer exists.

I tried to explain all this when I applied to be a part of the expedition. I described my regret as a researcher about not sharing my experiences in the field with others—particularly children and young people. I had told myself that I was so focused on my work that I just didn't have the time, but I knew this was a poor excuse—I just hadn't put the effort in, and it became a growing source of guilt.

Increasingly I recognized the importance of reporting what I had seen, and not just in terms of science. I could explain what I did in the field and why it was important but also impart those moments of revelation that had enabled me to see so clearly the urgency of our global situation. More than that, in sharing my story with young people, particularly from the rural region in northern France where I had been raised, I could prove to them that everything is possible in life. I envisioned that if selected to be part of the expedition to the North Pole, I would be evidence that a local girl from a small city in a part of France far from the sea and the mountains, surrounded by flat rural country and agricultural fields full of melons, could still make a difference by traveling the world to study marine mammals and even reach the top of the world on my skis with a global team.

I had always struggled to explain what I felt personally and why I had an urge to travel to such remote and inhospitable places, but I was sure that this expedition would give me the impetus to do what I knew I needed to do: to be a witness for those who may never get the opportunity to see Arctic Ocean sea ice or the glaciers of the Antarctic Peninsula for themselves.

Despite my enthusiasm, as I submitted my application I was doubtful I would be selected and even less convinced that I would cut it as a team member, even if I was picked. As a scientist, I had spent a lot of time in colder-than-average places where we didn't have many comforts. Field seasons often involved living in tents or huts made of old wooden boxes or even shipping containers where the only water supply for washing was melting the snow outside—but we always had a supply of bottled water for drinking, lots of food to keep us satisfied, and gas stoves to warm up the basic huts when needed. Occasionally I would be required to carry heavy equipment here and there, but usually the specific jobs of looking after such things as food, logistics, and setting up the base were assigned to someone else.

An Arctic ski expedition is totally different. Fieldwork never involved pulling a ninety-pound sledge for ten hours every day through an endless field of broken ice, as this expedition would require. I felt I had the mental toughness but I was really worried about the physical demands. When I thought of polar expeditions, what came to mind were the heroic and frequently deadly stories of the explorers of the nineteenth and twentieth centuries, men like Shackleton, Amundsen, and Scott. These stories left no doubt that in order to be a polar explorer you had to be superfit, strong and athletic, unfailingly stoic in all situations, and possessed of an inherent fortitude that fueled polar ability—and a freakish disregard for your extremities.

There is no map of the North Pole to study. There is no guide to how flat it might be or how big and how many the obstacles are—much less where. I had imagined the Arctic Ocean to be something like a frozen lake, but looking at images and films on the internet I could see that this wasn't the case at all. I wanted to know more about this unmappable place to familiarize myself with the terrain, but as I watched ice blocks turning over as if they were bobbing bath toys and great sheets of ice rising up out of open water to pile one on top of the other, I became more, rather than less, daunted.

I couldn't believe it when I discovered, while standing in my mother's garden, that Felicity had chosen me to be a member of the Women's Euro-Arabian North Pole Expedition. I couldn't help but cry tears of happiness. I didn't know what to do—I felt like screaming and laughing all at the same time. There was so much emotion. Me. Susan Gallon. Selected. Chosen. I was going to the North Pole! It had been a vague dream rolling around my mind for many years, and now Felicity had provided me with an opportunity not only to achieve that dream but to make it even bigger by sharing it with others.

NATAŠA: *I probably would never have applied for the expedition if we were exploring a jungle or a rain forest or anywhere with snakes and spiders. I also would have passed on the opportunity for an adventure that would take me really high up in the mountains, where I would need to face my fear of height. Just not my cup of tea. But cold? Skiing? Polar bears?* Well, that could be fun, *I was telling myself.*

Susan, from France

I come from the city of Kočevje, often referred to as Slovenia's Siberia because of its harsh climate. I know how it feels at -20°C (-4°F)—our winters are really cold! Admittedly this didn't give me any idea how it feels at the -40°C (-40°F) we could expect at the North Pole, but I could see at least a tiny connection with the expedition. My native Kočevsko region is wild. It's a place where you can become one with nature, breathe in fresh forest air, and listen to the sound of birds. The diverse landscape allows for a wide variety of adventures, as it is crisscrossed with a network of hiking and cycling trails. With beautiful mountains and picturesque lakes, many people find joy and happiness from being in this region.

I didn't know much about the Arctic before I applied for the *expedition. I feel embarrassed now that I often confused the Arctic with Antarctica geographically, never really certain which one was "below" and which "above"—but as I heard more about the presence of polar bears in the Arctic I saw another similarity with my home region. For Kočevsko is the home of the majestic brown bear. This most powerful animal of the forests can, with a little luck, still be seen simply while hiking along the trails.*

I made sure to mention the brown bear living in my native region when filling out the application for the expedition, hoping that this fact could perhaps suggest that I was experienced when meeting wild beasts—that I would not scream and panic if a polar bear crossed our path in the Arctic. For the same reason I also mentioned that Kočevje is one of the coldest places in Slovenia, but when asked what I was most afraid of, I honestly pointed out that it was the extreme cold we would face. I was aware that I risked being eliminated in the first round by this answer, and for this reason alone I hesitated to apply until just a few days before the application deadline.

I wasn't sure of my chances of selection, but not because I doubted my abilities. I emphasized my accomplished journalistic career and communication skills in the application, confident my proven expertise in using social media would be an asset for the success of the expedition. Rather, I was afraid that applicants from bigger countries—and therefore more attractive to possible sponsors—would have an advantage. I didn't think that I, coming from a small country, had even the slightest chance to be a part of the team. Assessing my prospects, I was aware that I hadn't done anything close to the enormous tasks and efforts this expedition demanded—but as a sports and, later, political affairs journalist, I had organized quite a few major projects, gaining some experience with organization and preparation on the way, which I hoped would work in my favor. What I felt was more important was that I am determined, reliable, and responsible, someone who the leader of the expedition could always count on doing her part. I hoped this would be enough. Ultimately, I decided I wanted to present myself as I truly am, phobia of the cold or no.

"You applied for an expedition to the North Pole? You? You don't like cold temperatures, cold water, cold anything. You are kidding, right?" This was the response from my sister and all of my friends when I told them about the application for the Women's Euro-Arabian North Pole Expedition. "You need 25°[C 80°F] to operate," someone said. Another told me, "You need twenty minutes to get ready to take a swim in the Adriatic—which is really warm." Everyone was puzzled and making fun of me. I could hear them laughing at the idea of me "conquering" the north, let alone imagining me going out there for real. I couldn't blame them for their reaction. At that time I was using feather-filled pillows and comforters all year round, hardly touching seawater if the temperature was below 25°C (80°F), zealously maintaining really warm temperatures in my apartment and running a "it's-hot-like-a-sauna-in-here" car heating system. As a self-proclaimed queen of heat, an expedition to the North Pole was not exactly in character.

"We really enjoyed reading your application form and it is clear that you would be a real asset as a potential team member. Therefore, we would really like to speak to you..."

Is this true? I asked myself as I reread Felicity's email. I was surprised by how excited and happy I felt to learn I was short-listed. A few weeks later, in the middle of the afternoon, Felicity called. I was in Paris, ready and prepared for the Skype call. Felicity had a very reassuring and calming voice when she was talking about the difficulties of traveling to the North Pole. She didn't paint a rosy picture, talking plainly about the dangers of the extreme cold, such as shifting ice blocks and potential encounters with polar bears. Her kindness in communication was completely enchanting. Regardless of the fact that I had absolutely no experience with that part of the

The first training camp on a glacier in Iceland. For some team members this was their first experience of cold, snow, and ice.

world and with any expedition, she talked to me as if we were equals. She acted encouragingly. Her plan was clear, and from the first communication onward I somehow trusted her, even though I hadn't even met her yet.

When she invited questions, I asked, "Would there be any possibility to send tweets or photos from the ice? Is there a satellite phone that would allow us to communicate and post photos on our social media?" I wasn't worried about extreme cold, polar bears, or ice shifting. The only real worry, aside from falling in the freezing water (yes, I was afraid of that), was how to find ways to share the expedition on the spot, on the ice, while we were moving. My main concern was to report from the North Pole to those who would be interested in following our progress.

My friend Teresa was in the room with me, listening to my conversation with Felicity. I could see her from the corner of my eye and knew that she was listening, nodding in my direction every now and then—and occasionally suppressing laughter. Teresa was the biggest supporter of my application, but as soon as I finished the call with Felicity she said, "What's wrong with you; are you crazy? You might get a special ticket for one of the most dangerous adventures out there,

traveling to the coldest place on Earth and all you are asking is if you would be able to tweet?"

I thought the interview had gone pretty well and that I'd done a good job at being convincing as a strong potential explorer. "I'm a journalist; it was the right thing to ask," I replied. "What would you want me to ask her? What kind of socks should I wear?" I guess my conversation with Felicity exposed my professional prejudice. I saw the expedition and its mission, first and foremost, as a great project to report. I can only assume Felicity must have agreed with my perspective because I received an email the very next day: "Dear teammate, welcome to the expedition! It was a true pleasure to meet you through Skype last week and I am convinced that you will not only be a valued member of the team, contributing vitally to the success of the expedition, but also a wonderful ambassador for all the cultural and wider aims of the project."

I had to stop to read the message properly. I read it twice. Read it for the third time and finally said to myself, Yup. You are going to the North Pole. Time to get yourself some warm underwear.

The team learning to ski together as a group on the glacier in Iceland

THREE

Glacier

In 2004, the year after I returned from my three-year posting at a research station in Antarctica, I organized an expedition to Iceland. It was the first time I had visited the small island nation on the very edge of the Arctic, and like many others before me I was astonished by the raw wildness of the landscape and the extremity of the weather. Though it is easily accessible in a couple of hours flying from northern Europe, traveling to Iceland is nevertheless like being transported to another world. The tops of the vast glaciers that cover a large proportion of the interior of the country can have the same feel, and present many of the same challenges, as a more geographically remote polar landscape. When conditions are right, it can be easy to imagine that you are skiing over the inland ice of Greenland or Antarctica's polar plateau.

Having selected the team for the North Pole virtually, I was eager to organize an opportunity for us all to meet in person as soon as possible so that we could begin the long process of transforming ourselves—a group of strangers—into a polar expedition team worthy of the North Pole. Iceland seemed an obvious location for that, and I spent much of the summer of 2016 communicating with the team online as we set about finding the means, as a group, to fund a training expedition there.

It is one thing to promise commitment and determination when applying for a place on an expedition, and quite another to remember those promises during the long months of logistics and organization that follow—so I was gratified to find that many of the group were immediately proactive and demonstrated their dedication to being involved in every aspect of making the expedition a success. Asma emerged as a powerhouse of administration, drawing on her professional expertise in marketing to produce documents that focused our efforts and kept records of our progress. I had few opportunities to communicate with her directly, but I got a sense of her calm authority through the perfection of her PowerPoints and commanding spreadsheets.

Nataša, too, came to the fore. From the moment I met her on a video call to Paris, she had exuded confidence. I remember clearly that what was supposed to be her interview had almost immediately felt like my interrogation. After the call, I knew I would be a fool to miss the opportunity to capitalize on Nataša's expertise in the media world, but more so her no-nonsense ability to drive a project forward. It turned out to be one of my best decisions as I quickly came to know that I could rely on her, always, to be a voice of unstinting objectivity and reason—even if it wasn't exactly what I wanted to hear.

Together, we created an online crowdfunding campaign and were soon incredibly humbled by the generous support of friends, colleagues, and strangers alike who all wanted to see our ambitious project succeed. We owe a huge debt of gratitude to the many who showed such belief in us before we had produced any reason to inspire such faith. As a result, that autumn the team was able to gather in Iceland from our respective nations spread across all of Europe and the Middle East for our first training expedition. I arranged for us to spend our initial few days together in two large adjacent holiday cottages on the relatively mild south coast of the country. The remote location was surrounded by green fields and views of the sea, somewhere we could get to know each other and do basic training before we ventured inland and onto the nearby glacier of Langjökull.

It was with a considerable degree of anticipation that I finally met my new team in person for the first time. After months of communicating online, everyone was simultaneously familiar and a stranger. I knew their turn of speech and the details of their lives and yet not their mannerisms, the way they moved or laughed. It was a little like meeting up with childhood friends after decades apart—known but alien at the same time. Even those among the group that I had counted as personal friends before the expedition I was now getting to know in a new context.

I'd first met Steph a decade earlier, when she had applied to be the Cypriot representative on an international ski expedition I was organizing to the South Pole. During her initial interview she had entered the room like a force of nature, and I immediately felt as if she was someone I had known forever—but I was also struck by her default language of self-deprecation. Almost every thought she shared focused on what she perceived as her faults or failings. Her self-doubt resonated with me. At that time I was putting together what would be my first major polar expedition, and the pressure of carrying the confidence and expectations of so many had taken its toll. My self-doubt had often become debilitating and I had needed to work hard to quieten those destructive internal voices.

Over the two-year project that followed, Steph emerged as one of the most determined, self-disciplined, and dependable members of the Antarctica team. Just as the success of that expedition taught me some much-needed self-belief, it was apparent that it had also given Steph renewed confidence in herself. I needed Steph to be involved in this new endeavor, and not just because I was aware she had longed for another polar adventure and the cherished bonds of camaraderie that

had come with it; it was also because she had been through the process of going from zero experience of the polar world to successfully
completing a tough polar journey, in much the same way as I was now
asking of my new team. I hoped the group might draw reassurance and
confidence from Steph's experiences and that she would be a constant
proof that what I was asking of them was possible.

Ahead of everyone's arrival, I had prepared sessions on every aspect
of our venture, from science and nutrition to clothing, fitness, and
all-important mental preparation. Drawing on what I had learned from
previous expeditions, we held indoor discussions followed by time outdoors putting theory into practice—pitching tents, lighting stoves, or
using GPS units to navigate small test courses around the local area.
Equally important to these practical skills, however, were the efforts
made to establish a sense of trust and common purpose between us.
I had asked everyone to bring something of their home with them to
Iceland, and over dinner on our first night together we learned about
the Slovenian love of honey and the ritual surrounding Arabic coffee,
sampling the homemade blend of Asma's grandmother.

Most evenings I posed a question to the group and during dinner
we would take turns to answer.

"What's the coldest temperature you've ever experienced?" I asked
one night.

"Right here at this table with that Icelandic draft blowing through
the door!" someone replied jokingly.

Other answers were more revealing. To the question "When have
you felt most adventurous in your life?" Misba told a story of climbing
in the Atlas Mountains of Morocco, while Nataša spoke of her time as
a political correspondent in Washington covering the election of President Obama. But Mariam shared a story about learning to ride a bike.

"There's no law in Saudi Arabia that says women can't ride a bike,"
she said, "and yet it is not something you see." She told us how she

had asked her male colleague one day if she could borrow his bike, remembering how much she had enjoyed cycling as a child. Gradually, short rides around local streets became longer journeys passing other pedestrians and gliding alongside cars. "I could tell people were surprised and almost speechless at times," she recalled. "But the overall reaction I received was of support. Some people even cheered."

Other women asked to join her, and Mariam's cycling evolved into a regular women's group going for weekly rides along the coast of the Red Sea early on Friday mornings, when the streets were empty. "It felt so empowering," she said. "We would get thumbs-up from strangers, and men asking if their wives or daughters could join us. I never imagined that a simple desire to ride a bike, and going for it, could be so powerful."

One morning her cycling group was stopped by a police officer. He told them that he personally had no problem with the group riding bikes, but he was sure that it wasn't "right." He called his superior, who showed up a few minutes later—and who then called *his* superior. "Pretty soon the big boss arrived," Mariam told us. "As soon as he got out of his car and saw five grown women with bicycles surrounded by cops, he started laughing. I knew then that everything would be fine. Women cycling is a new sight to see in Saudi but people are ready for the change. We just need to normalize it."

Those cozy nights filled with inspiring stories were soon replaced with a daunting reality check. We left the green fields of the coast behind and traveled inland, up to the elevated polar-like terrain of Langjökull and straight into the dull gloom of a whiteout. For most of the team it was the first time they had ever experienced this environment or conditions like it, but falling back on what we had learned together over the previous days, three tents were quickly pitched and everyone huddled inside.

I had allocated the grouping for each tent based on spreading the previous experience within the team evenly and balancing character types based on what I had seen throughout our first few days together. For example, I noted that Anisa and Ida—similar in age and confidence, both athletic and used to being in charge—appeared to gravitate toward one another during the outdoor practical sessions. Whenever I spotted a natural resonance between people I tried to capitalize on it, figuring that these connections were probably stronger than anything I could artificially inspire. Time would tell whether my judgment had been successful, and I expected to make adjustments over time, if not.

I shared a tent with Nataša and Mariam and was relieved to find

Misba (left) and Felicity

that Nataša's assurance and Mariam's calm created a very self-suffi-cient and capable unit that seemed to need very little support from me. I really appreciated how they gave me space in the evenings to attend to the other demands on my time. I never felt under any pres-sure from them to chat or to be the leader when it was just the three of us. They seemed to understand that sometimes I returned to the tent mentally exhausted and needed to be a passive beneficiary of their conversation and humor. I particularly noted their efforts to resolve any problem they had themselves rather than burden me with it. They were trying to lighten my load and I was both touched and grateful.

That said, it's easy to get comfortable inside the warm bubble of a tent and to draw a sense of safety and protection from it—but the safety is an illusion. You are in many ways more vulnerable when inside a tent because you are oblivious to changes in the environment outside—such as a brewing storm, a crack in the ice, or an approaching polar bear. Worse, there is a tendency to cling to that perceived safety and shrink from the challenge outside. The weather always sounds a lot worse from within and can provide a convincing reason to stay put rather than venture out. It's an insidious inertia that can be hard to shake off.

My novice team needed to know that we could face whatever con-ditions waited for us, and I wanted to lessen the fear of the specter it had already formed in their minds. As darkness fell I asked everyone to gather outside for a ski lesson. It was an unpopular request. Many on the team were still getting to know me, both as a person and as a lead-er, and we didn't have any trust between us yet. Nevertheless, despite their misgivings, the whole team was soon outside and on their skis. After some brief technique advice we set off in shaky circuits around the camp by the light of our headlamps, those with experience instinc-tively helping those who had never had skis on their feet before. Not only was it dark and cold but the wind was propelling hard, icy snow horizontally into our faces—a specialty of Icelandic glaciers.

We eventually drifted back to the tents, and the shift in the atmosphere around camp couldn't have been more striking. It was as if a spell had been broken. Trepidation and doubt were replaced by a sense of satisfaction at having endured something that had seemed so daunting. The team had been through a moment of what had felt like adversity together, and that shared experience accelerated our bonding as a group. Those who had been worried about how they would perform—especially when exposed to the difficulties of the glacier—were reassured, and we had all witnessed how we could function successfully together. It built some trust, in ourselves and in each other. In the chatter and giggles that radiated out into the darkness from the tents that evening, I heard the clear sound of a breath that had been collectively held being suddenly released. It was relief, and it marked the beginning of our transformation into an expedition team.

Returning to my tent that evening, I felt vindicated. The unpopular ski session had been the right decision, though I remained wary of pushing too hard, worried that if I got the balance wrong I could demolish confidence rather than build it. The next morning, Lara from Jordan told me she didn't wish to continue as part of the expedition. It was immediately clear that her decision was already final and that for me to try and change her mind would be to risk having a member of the team who felt coerced into being there.

Sorry as I was to lose Lara—she had brought much energy and laughter to the group—and to lose the association with her country, I nevertheless appreciated the courage and self-knowledge it must have taken for her to make the choice. It is often so much harder to stop than to allow ourselves to be carried along. I respected her honesty, too. She did not try to find an excuse but simply stated the truth: she wasn't enjoying the experience and wanted to go home. Even so, as I drove Lara off the glacier I wondered if the outcome would have been any different if I hadn't insisted on the pitch-dark ski lesson.

A pitch-dark ski lesson in a blizzard on the summit of an Icelandic glacier was a controversial start for the team.

STEPH: *The drive to the south of Iceland from the country's international airport is a long but scenic one. To the right, glimpses of the gray agitated sea; to my left, free-form hills of lava rock disappearing into low ragged clouds. I saw a lot of moss. There weren't many cars or signs on the road. Tightly packed into a minivan for our first training expedition, it felt like we were on a girl's road trip, albeit one overloaded with winter gear, skis, and lots of junk food. I couldn't* help but feel a degree of sympathy for my new expedition teammates. Most of them had no idea what awaited them: expedition training, endless logistics spreadsheets, the stress of looking for sponsorship, and ultimately being in the most extreme environment in the world. I was no expert, but I felt comforted to have already experienced all of this before.

Thanks to social media, I already knew who everyone was and had become relatively accustomed to their faces. Anisa from Oman was easy to identify. She had huge, densely curled, mahogany hair, which was impressively voluminous even when tied back in a ponytail. She gave the impression of being confident and looked very fit. I learned that she worked as an outdoor activity instructor in Oman and spent most of her time in the desert, off grid. I made a mental note that she should have useful map-reading skills and an ability to work with tents and stoves.

Nataša from Slovenia, with distinctive short blonde hair, and Susan from France seemed to have formed a close friendship already, probably from having spent time together during their long layover in Oslo Airport on the way to Iceland. I introduced myself to Ida from Sweden. She had lived in Svalbard, worked in Antarctica, and knew how to use a rifle. I felt a bit awestruck, instantly understanding why Felicity would select such a strong candidate to join the team. Ida already knew my connection to Felicity and seemed eager to inform me that she was experienced on skis and with Hilleberg tents, which are Swedish. My Middle Eastern teammates were rapidly bonding, chatting animatedly to each other in Arabic, gesticulating wildly and laughing. Lara from Jordan and Asma from Qatar looked very polished, even in shapeless winter expedition gear. I made a mental note to use eyeliner more often.

Arriving at the two wooden cottages that were to be home for the next week, I felt thankful to be sharing a room with Felicity. I was unexpectedly overwhelmed by the sheer size of the team. It was a relief to close the door finally and have some quiet time to myself. I lay awake for a while trying to process everything, wondering whether this team of strangers would ever form those lasting bonds that I treasured from my time in Antarctica.

I wondered, too, where I would fit in. I knew Felicity wanted me to draw on my past experience to help her with the administration involved in running a large expedition team, but I was also supposed to be a sort of reassurance to the team members who had never done anything like this before. I was worried that a long expedition hiatus had left me lacking. Self-doubt burned red-hot in my ears.

The first day of training reinforced my fears. Lighting the palm-sized camping stoves used in the tents had always been my least favorite task. My heart dropped when it was my turn to practice in front of the group. With increasing frustration I wasn't able to light the stove properly. My hands trembled, and the tentacles of self-doubt that had first emerged the night before began to take a tight grip on my mind. The same fear I had felt ten years ago when learning to use the stoves for the first time returned. The lit match in my hand suddenly ignited a drop of liquid fuel in the base of the metal stove and a flame exploded upward, curling into a red hand, its fingers stretching out to reach my face and singe my eyebrows. I could feel everyone's eyes on me. Embarrassment made me burn hotter than the flame I was failing to get under control.

Felicity walked past and, ignoring my helpless look, muttered, "Come on, Steph. You know how to do this."

Do I, though? I asked myself.

I couldn't shake the feeling that I was pushing my luck being on another expedition and that I had no right to be there. The thought deepened as I watched Misba from Manchester, a mother of two with no previous expedition experience, take her turn lighting the stove and reveal herself to be a natural. Everyone proved their worth on the team one way or another as we progressed through the training. Nataša used to be a journalist and was now a social media guru, so *she used her knowledge to teach us how to be more effective with our online expedition presence. Asma, a member of the Qatar Olympic Committee, explained to us in detail about sponsorship and marketing. Even quiet, shy Lamees from Kuwait, who had been very much in the background and alone, obviously preferring to be an observer rather than a participant, showed us some of her animation work as a graphic designer and was tasked to conjure up a meaningful expedition logo.*

I felt slightly more assured when we moved from the cottages to the glacier. I was back in a polar environment, and when Felicity told us we were going to ski in the whiteout, I was pleased. As I clipped on my skis, the tension of the last week dissolved.

It was windy and cold, the snow falling relentlessly in big wet flakes that froze into a hard crust on every surface. Pulling the hood of my waterproof jacket tightly over my head and arranging my fleecy neck gaiter to cover my nose, I disappeared behind my ski goggles to observe the scene around me. In the dark, it was impossible to tell who was who, despite the headlamps everyone was wearing. All I could see were silhouettes. Someone slipped and fell over their skis. Someone else got cold and broke out of our single-line formation to stamp their feet and propel their arms to warm up. I began to remember how it felt to be my polar self once again, confidence trickling into me with each jog of my expedition memory.

Ida and Susan slid by with a hiss of ski edges on ice. They were the team members with the most skiing experience, and it showed: their pace was steady and smooth. Asma, Anisa, Nataša, and Lamees were making determined attempts to stay upright for as long as possible using their ski poles for balance, while Misba, Mariam, and Lara struggled more, wobbling on their skis with unsteady legs. Lara in particular was falling regularly, slipping on the uneven ice that was almost invisible in the bad weather and finding it hard to keep her balance. Everyone eagerly called out encouragement, but it only seemed to make her frustration worse. I could see that frustration slowly turning to anger.

I looked beyond the group, toward the dark outline of our tents pitched nearby, almost obscured by the heavy, wind-driven snow. This was a baptism by fire for many of the team, most of whom had never skied before, never mind on the summit of an Arctic glacier, in the dark and through a blizzard. It was a brutal introduction, and I found myself wondering how many of my new teammates would wake after our first night in the tents unwilling to give it another go.

Felicity had decided who would be sharing a tent together. I was allocated a tent with Lara, Susan, and Lamees. I was worried at first that we might make a rather sullen grouping, but once back in the tent the chatter came easily. Lamees was an identical twin; Lara's daughter was on the national football squad; and Susan, through her science work, had visited some of the most remote places in the world to study seals. Outside I could hear stoves roaring in the other tents and chatter like our own rising out into the night, and I felt comfort in that first tug of new camaraderie.

The next morning, however, there was a clear shift in the mood around camp. I'd shivered through most of the night and suspected everyone else had too. Glancing at Susan's thermometer, I saw it had dropped to -10°C (14°F) during the night. There was a thick layer of ice on the inside of the tent, created by the moisture in our breath freezing. Susan and I carefully shook the fabric of the tent, trying to avoid the ice falling onto our sleeping bags. We both noticed that Lara had been silent since getting out of our sleeping bags.

"I'm done," she announced in a firm voice, holding her knitted bobble hat and black liner gloves ready in her hand. "It's not for me."

Her face had a fixed look of conviction as she explained it was being away from her family as much as the cold that had swayed her. We all tried to change her mind, but it was clear that she was determined. As

Lamees started talking to her in Arabic, I wondered what I could have done differently to help Lara enjoy the experience more. Could I have offered more reassurance? Could I have done something to keep her spirits up? It made little difference now.

By the time we set off for our first full day skiing over the glacier, arrangements had been made for Lara to return to the coast and start her travel home. I'd barely had time to get to know her, yet her departure still left a hole. Within our tent group of four we had already split the jobs we needed to get done every evening and morning, such as preparing meals and gathering snow blocks to melt for water. We had already established a routine for pitching the tent that involved four pairs of hands, and now we would have to adapt to being just three. Lara and Lamees had taken charge of making the inside of the tent homey. Now all of that would fall to Lamees. I wondered what other impacts Lara's departure might turn out to have on our fledgling team.

The Icelandic glacier rewarded our first sleepless night with the most stunning of days. For the first time it was clear that we were on top of an elevated cap of ice surrounded by mountains, with expansive views in all directions. The ice sparkled in the sunshine with the brilliance of millions of diamonds, like the Mediterranean Sea glistening in the afternoon sun. It crunched loudly under the weight of our sledges and skis as we moved in a straight line toward the curvature of the white plane beyond. Ida and I broke out of the line of skiers to take photos. Left behind for a moment, we grinned at each other and, laughing, expressed elaborate gratitude to the Icelandic weather gods for the lovely day before racing back to join the line that was already looking like a trail of ants in the distance. Everyone's tiredness seemed wiped away, replaced with chatter and sprinkled with laughter.

We had planned to stop for a longer lunch break to give some of my teammates the opportunity to pray. While most of us sat on our sledges to eat from snack bags in our pockets and drink from insulated flasks

The bad weather cleared and the team woke to a new world on the glacier. Eventually the views stretched for miles.

fished out of our sledge bags, Misba and Lamees covered their heads with a thin white scarf over the top of their skiing gear and knelt in the snow a little way from the group. I had been aware of my Muslim teammates disappearing to pray regularly throughout the training, but it had always been something done in private. This was the first time it had been done among the rest of the team, and we became hushed in respect, even though no one had required, or asked for, silence. I watched my teammates bowing in prayer in the sparkly white nature of the glacier plateau, and my lungs filled with air that felt pure and crisp. I was surprised by the spirituality of the moment. It was an instant of peace and contentment that I knew would stay with me.

LAMEES: *I arrived at the airport for our first expedition training alone but spotted the team easily—a noisy concentration of laughter and excited faces sitting together in a coffee shop next to a telltale mound of rucksacks and outdoor gear. I had seen images of everyone and chatted to some through a computer screen, but seeing them all together in real life at last was like stepping into a hurricane of positive vibes. When Felicity arrived at the airport to collect us, she pulled up in the most enormous bright orange truck I have ever seen. Its wheels were the height of my waist. I realized then that this was going to be a most unusual trip.*

Felicity didn't say much at first. She seemed determined to stick to her schedule, but we were already behind. The plan was to spend a few days in a cluster of cottages on the south coast of Iceland, where it was autumnal but still relatively warm, before moving to Langjökull ("long glacier") to camp on snow and ice in expedition conditions.

During those first days of the training, I woke each morning in a swirl of new information and mingled impressions, thinking, Where am I? But it was a wonderful experience to be learning so much in such a short time. One morning we learned how to use the specialized clothing, another how to use the handheld GPS units and about navigation, or lighting the small stoves that burn liquid fuel, melting ice to make water, even pitching the tents and organizing ourselves to share the restricted space among four people.

I thrived on the routine of it all and loved the spirit of the team, the heartening feel of everyone working together, but whenever I got a chance I liked to go off on my own and find a private venture. I had never been to Iceland before, and I wanted to make sure I made the most of it. Despite the Icelandic weather and exhausting program, I

The northern lights blooming across the night sky during the team's stay in huts on the south coast of Iceland

forced myself several times to go on an early run before our trainings. I ran through still-green fields backed by tree-covered hillsides. The trees were all turning a bright marigold yellow that stood out against the heavy gray sky.

I was sorry to see such thick clouds, as I was desperate to see the northern lights. Each evening I would keep a close eye on the sky, but it wasn't until our last night in the cottages that we finally had a clear night full of stars. I knew it was my best chance to spot the aurora borealis and was determined not to miss it. I found a dark, sheltered spot outside the cottage, away from any light, to sit and watch the heavens. Eventually the rest of the team went to bed but I stayed on,

*observing the night. At one in the morning I was rewarded with a bloom
of green amongst the stars. There it was—the aurora! I rushed inside
the cottage, calling everyone outside to see, before returning to watch
as particles were accelerated across the sky, leaving waves and stripes
of color like magic. The colors varied from green to pink and white, and
the complexity of the dance became ever more interesting. It lasted only
for a matter of minutes but was spellbinding.*

*The next morning the wonder of the night was swept away by cold
and gloom. As we left the cottages and headed to the glacier, my mood*

**The team setting up their camp in snow and ice for the very first time.
Felicity is on the far left.**

began to match the weather. The green fields disappeared and were replaced with moonlike landscapes of rock as we climbed up toward the ice. Eventually all I could see were varying shades of dirty white, from the thick cloud cover to the gray-looking snow. Noticing us starting to huddle together in the back of the truck and put on extra layers, Felicity explained that the temperature would drop the higher and farther north we went.

The moment we stepped out of the protective bubble of the truck onto the ice will be forever engraved in my memory. It was cold, windy, and white. We were in the middle of a snow storm and I could barely see anything. The snow stuck to every surface and blew painfully into my eyes. In no time my beloved woolly hat was sodden and useless. It wasn't meant for this kind of weather! I tried to remain calm, and after what felt like an age I was finally able to crawl into the shelter of the tent. I was soaked with snow. My hair was wet, my hat frozen, and my hands as cold as stone. I could feel myself shivering. I took off my shoes awkwardly in the cramped space at the entrance of the tent. I heard the girls asking me to take off my jacket immediately as it was filled with snow. Too many instructions! *my head complained.* Too many details! Just leave me alone to get warm.

Inside, I wedged myself into a corner of the tent and sat there saying nothing. No one was saying anything. As we looked at each other in silence I could see the discomfort in my companions' faces, and I imagined my own showed the same. I stared glumly at the pathetic little mound of belongings in my allocated corner of the tent in the wet and the cold. The tent suddenly felt very small and the challenges of sharing this restricted space loomed large in my mind with new reality.

What have I done? *I asked myself.* How am I going to survive another five days of this?

Someone turned on the small camping stove we kept at one end of the tent and started melting snow to prepare hot chocolate. As minuscule wafts of warmth slowly filled the tent, our will seemed to return to us a little. We began to dry out our clothes and prepare some food and even to chat, just to ease some of the discomfort and shock. I had no idea that the challenge of the evening had just begun. An hour later the door of the tent peeled open and Felicity appeared from the dark. She sat with the tent door zipped around her to keep out the worst of the snow, half of her leaning inward. Her appearance was like a sudden tear in the fragile bubble of comfort we had managed to muster. She asked us to get our headlamps and meet outside in five minutes.

Why are we meeting outside? *I thought to myself in panic.* Couldn't we just call it a night and tomorrow I promise I will be the first in line?

I understand now, in hindsight, that the harder the training, the easier the experience when it comes to the real thing, but at the time it felt like an unnecessary madness—almost cruelty. Getting out of the tent, even with my headlamp on, it felt dark, really dark. All I could see was a spot of light from my lamp on the ice-covered ground ahead of me, dimmed by thick snow falling in the beam. I joined a huddle of figures, faces covered with our proper winter gear as we had been taught, skis on, poles in hand.

"Lamees, you will be first in line," Felicity called through the darkness.

I had never skied in my life, ever, and now she wanted me to be the first in line, in minimal visibility? It was hard to see how my situation could get any worse, but I said nothing and instead concentrated on the long cross-country skis attached to my feet. They were as long as I was high and not even as wide as my boots. I slid forward over uneven snow, keeping myself steady with the long ski poles that came up almost as far as my shoulders. At first it was difficult to get any rhythm going between skis and poles, as my hair was protruding from my hat. Untied, it blew repeatedly across my face; my scarf wasn't tucked in properly and got tangled, and my outer jacket wasn't fully zipped up, with the result that it was slowly filling with thick falling snow. I stopped to sort myself out and made a mental note—next time I would make sure to prepare myself and my clothing properly before clipping into my skis. I needed to be able to focus on the effort of moving forward and nothing else. My worst fear was to find myself to be the one slowing down the team. The thought of the others waiting for me filled me with horror.

Think fast and move fast, *I told myself over and over. Once I had pulled myself together, I found I quickly gained confidence on the skis and the rhythm came naturally. By the time we got back into the tent I was actually enjoying myself. I felt refreshed! And relieved. Wriggling into my sleeping bag for the night feeling warm and well-pleased with my performance for the day, I went to sleep telling myself,* Four days left, Lamees. Four days. You can do this. You can do this.

MISBA: *I was assigned to a tent with Ida (who was very experienced), as well as Asma and Anisa. They were all much younger, and I was disappointed not to be in a tent with Lara. Early on my new tent-mates decided that I would take on the role of chef. I would look after the "kitchen" in the tent with responsibility for managing the stove and melting snow to make water for everyone. When I asked them why, they said, "Because you are the team mama."*

I accepted the role. I didn't speak up to say no. But the stove scared me. It was a small thing that could fit in the palm of my hand, and it used liquid fuel that was stored in a small bottle attached to the stove by a thin pipe. A little of the fuel had to be leaked into the stove and lit until it warmed up the pipe and turned the remaining fuel into gas that could be lit. I'd never had to use anything like it before, and it was a challenging job to master. Not only did you have to light it; once lit, the flow of fuel had to be managed carefully so that the flames didn't go out or, more importantly, flare up and ignite the tent. I was terrified of burning a hole in the expensive expedition tents that would be our home on the ice during the real expedition.

I was also intimidated by the skiing. When we traveled to Langjökull to learn how to cross-country ski, Felicity assured me that "cross-country skiing on the glacier is not so much skiing as scrambling." But I sensed the rest of the team was also realizing, perhaps for the first time like me, exactly what we were letting ourselves in for. That first night it was dark and freezing cold. By the light of our headlamps, we learned how to ski across the icy, undulating, unyielding surface of the glacier. In a long line we made endless figure eights across the alien landscape—for three hours!

Returning to the tents provided little respite; sleeping on the glacier was torture. Lying with just a couple of foam mats and one layer of

Moody light and plenty of ice greeted the team on their first morning on the glacier after experiencing a very cold night in the tents.

a sleeping bag between me and the ice of the glacier, I could feel the cold creeping through my back and into my bones. Ida told me, "You're always going to be cold, never warm." The thought of never being warm made me despair. I longed to feel warm in my sleeping bag as I remembered feeling on other trips. I wanted the relief and comfort of being toasty and falling to sleep in peace. Now I didn't look forward to sleep, knowing what a tortured experience it would be. Surprisingly, though, I never suffered from aches and pains due to my age, which I had expected; I was just very cold. For the first two days on the glacier I scarcely ever spoke in the evening. I was simply trying to acclimatize mentally as well as physically.

We woke at seven and I made the breakfast and melted water for each of my tent-mates for the day—my role as chef. Then we had to get all our gear on, take down the tents, and pack the sledges before leaving at nine. Some of us were quicker than others that first day, and those who were left standing idly out in the cold waiting for the last tent to pack up got annoyed. At the North Pole such a delay could result in hypothermia, we were told. We had to do better.

We set off half an hour late for our first ninety-minute ski. It was the first time I had hauled a heavy sledge behind me. Others in the group who were more experienced passed on advice and the mantra "lift and glide, lift and glide," which I repeated to myself continuously. Skiing took all my concentration and was much more physically demanding than I had imagined. None of the Arab teammates had been on skis, either, but they were younger and quicker at learning. I kept myself going by singing to myself or talking out loud, mumbling into my buff. We skied all day in ninety-minute intervals with seven-minute breaks in between. In the breaks we all had to eat something and drink water, and in the longer midday break I could pray.

That first full day on the glacier, we skied thirteen miles. As we pitched the tents I was determined to light the stove that evening all by myself—but once again, I had to ask for help. Later we sat in the tent sipping the hot chocolate I had made for everyone, and I listened to the others talk about their experiences of the day. We were all exhausted and cold, but I clearly wasn't adapting to the temperature as easily as everyone else. I seemed to feel the cold a lot more.

When Felicity told us that Lara was leaving, I was stunned. She had seemed so confident, and people listened when she spoke. How could she be quitting the team? If she was not going to complete the training, how could I expect to? I hurried over to the truck where Lara sat, all ready to leave. "Are you sure this is what you want?" I asked her. She explained that she was quite sure. I have to confess that I was more than a little tempted to join her—but then I thought of those thousand women who had applied unsuccessfully to join this extraordinary expedition, and I gritted my teeth and determined to carry on. It surely couldn't get any harder. Could it?

The Sugar Dunes along the Sea of Oman, so pale they could be snow

FOUR

Desert

As the team dispersed after our training expedition in Iceland, we resumed our well-established mode of online communication. We now faced the daunting and often demoralizing task of raising the considerable funds needed to cover the costs of a North Pole expedition. Rather than each member being responsible for finding her own contribution, we set out to find corporate sponsorship for the expedition as a whole.

With our planned departure for the North Pole still more than eighteen months away, I knew that I also needed to plan another training expedition to maintain the momentum of the project and the enthusiasm of the team. While brainstorming suitable locations for the spring of 2017, I had an interesting idea…

Taking a polar expedition to prepare in the desert of the Arabian Peninsula was unusual, to say the least—but Oman turned out to be an ideal training location. We could develop our stamina and endurance equally well in any environment—pulling a sledge over sand on foot was, after all, very similar to dragging a sledge over snow on skis—but more importantly, the shifting landscape of desert dunes was as unmappable and as riven with unknowns as the ice of the Arctic Ocean. Uncertainty is a tough scenario to train for, and yet the ability to adapt

61

to never being sure what you are going to face the next day or the next hour, never being able to plan with any confidence, is an essential expedition skill.

On the sea ice, not knowing where or how often we would meet major obstacles made it difficult to anticipate how we might progress, how many days of food and fuel we would need, and even when our next stop might be. The same was true in the desert. It was impossible to predict what dunes you would meet or the best route to take. We had little idea how long we might be walking or how much water we would need. The uncertainty doesn't just affect the practical ability to plan but can eat away at morale too. Adapting to constant change can be hard if not practiced, just like any other skill.

Even so, the idea of mounting an expedition in the desert gave me pause. The polar environment is extreme but it is an extremity that has become familiar to me. In contrast, I knew nothing about traveling on foot across a desert. Without any experience to fall back on, I wasn't sure what equipment we would need or the best systems to follow. I sought advice from experts I trusted, but this didn't stop anxiety and nerves from nagging at my thoughts, amplifying insecurities and leading me to ask the same type of questions novice team members asked me before setting out into the cold—should I have brought a few extra sets of socks with me? Did I have a large enough water bottle? Would the terrain be navigable in the way I imagined? It was a timely reminder of how it must feel for those with little polar experience when they ventured out onto the ice for the first time, and how disorienting it is to try something new. I never allowed myself to forget the courage of my teammates in choosing to join the expedition and jumping feet first into the deepest of deep ends.

When skiing across a vast plain of polar snow, I have often squinted against the view to help me imagine that the crystals of ice reflecting the light all around me like a carpet of stars are in fact the sparkling white sands of a Caribbean beach. I indulge in this illusion to will myself to feel tropical warmth. In Oman I had the exact opposite experience. The Sugar Dunes of the coast were so pale that several times I looked around me and imagined a polar desert—and willed myself to feel the reviving chill of the poles.

Until Oman, despite my best efforts, the expedition project had been undeniably Eurocentric. We had only met in Europe, the website was only partially translated into Arabic, and English was our default language. Now, as we sat close together in a small patch of hastily erected shade, backs against the tires of the support vehicles, toes dug into the cooler layer of sand beneath the surface and faces turned eagerly into scant desert winds, we began to open up more to Arabic influence.

The points of crossover were as surprising as the evolving character of our team—scraps of our various cultures stitched together to create a team culture all our own. This patchwork of common reference ranged from the mundane to the profound. Lamees taught us how to wind long scarfs around our heads to keep off the sun. Anisa revealed the social and practical reasons to drink scalding hot Arabic coffee, even in the heat of the day. We adopted the versatile Arabic word *yalla*, most often used in multiples and variously with hand-waving, head-shaking, fist-pumping, or exclamation. Depending on the tone, it could mean "Let's go!" or "Get a move on!" It could be a form of encouragement or an expression of frustration. Accompanied by a sigh, it could even be a term of lament.

Mariam had recently attended her brother's marriage ceremony, and we listened, incredulous, as she filled one afternoon rest break with descriptions of the celebration. The length, complexity, and cost of a typical Saudi wedding were mind-blowing. The various days of different festivities involved didn't sound like an event—it was an entire season.

"My father has asked if I could try not to get married for a while," she said at the end of her description. I imagined he needed time for his constitution as well as his finances to recover. Mariam told us that her grandmother had been one of four wives and had said it was like having three sisters. Anisa's father also had more than one wife, including her mother. "By law," Anisa told us, "each wife must be treated exactly equally. The house of each wife must be the same size, and if one wife is bought a car, all the wives must have a new car. Everything must be the same." Both Anisa and Mariam spoke of the tradition positively, almost with nostalgia, but when Nataša asked if they would themselves consent to being a multiple wife, they firmly said no.

I was left with the impression that my Arabic teammates were navigating a cultural balancing act as constantly shifting as the dunes that surrounded us. There was not only the interplay of Arabic tradition and Western influence but also the steering of new thinking through the obstacle course of convention to find a new equilibrium. It also occurred to me that we were all facing this same challenge of change, one way or another. Women are most heavily impacted by much societal change and yet, frustratingly, are still relatively rarely in significant positions of influence over that change. I believe it is this fundamental disenfranchisement that needs to alter determinedly if the world is to move closer to an ideal of gender equality.

My motivation in putting together the expedition had been to develop a better understanding of the values and perspectives of women from different cultures, in the belief that greater knowing and greater mutual support between women are a way for everyone to make progress. But in establishing and leading that project, I discovered just as much about the influence my own culture had over the way I thought and acted. Even so, it was a surprise that the person on the team I felt most culturally distanced from was my fellow Brit, Misba. As she described the concerns within her community, and even her family, that required her consideration so that she could be who she was, I realized how little I knew about her reality despite having the same nationality. I began to see that cultural perspective—whether Middle Eastern or European—is the same everywhere in its inconsistency and diversity. The insight deepened my belief in the importance of continually creating opportunities to listen and share and question our own perceptions.

We also discovered that our willingness to understand ended firmly at our stomachs. Food is a wonderful form of cultural exchange, but where we differed irreconcilably turned out to be humble peanut butter. I was in charge of designing and preparing the rations for our Omani training expedition. On the day I prepared peanut butter and jam sandwiches—with banana slices—Misba and Nataša turned on me. "What are you feeding us?" they demanded. I consider the combination of jam, banana, and peanut butter to be nutritionally brilliant for a training diet, but I found little support among the team. They each professed never to have been given anything quite as unforgivably inedible in all their lives.

They say the way to someone's heart is through their stomach—it turns out that it is also a good way to earn someone's permanent distrust.

LAMEES: *We had all met in Muscat, the capital of Oman, before a 150-mile drive to the Wahiba Sands, a perfect desert landscape of uninterrupted dunes. Arriving just before midnight, we were all exhausted from the journey, and we did little more than grab some food and put up the tents before gratefully dropping into our sleeping bags. I fell asleep with a big smile on my face, thankful to be experiencing a new flavor of wilderness. But I didn't realize that we had already made our first mistake.*

The next morning, I woke with the sun in my eyes, feeling my skin on fire and soaked in sweat. In our exhaustion the night before we had pitched our tents facing east so that the white-hot morning sun came right into our faces, bearing down on the entrance of our tent. It was so hot inside that I felt drowsy and desperate to leave to seek some shade. Outside we met other teammates who had made the same mistake. Even in this environment, which I knew so well and loved so much, I still had a lot to learn.

Together the team gradually established a routine. We'd wake at six and after making breakfast, preparing snack bags, and filling water bottles, we'd set off around seven. Each of us dragged a small plastic sledge weighted with camping equipment attached to a padded harness around our waists. Dragging the sledge over sand felt much as it had over snow in Iceland. We didn't have skis, but some of the team walked with ski poles. We tried to stick to the hour-and-a-half legs that had worked so well previously, but we added quick water breaks every fifteen minutes as well as the constant application of sunscreen.

At one in the afternoon the temperatures became too hot to continue, so we got into the habit of building a shelter and having a rest until the sun cooled down around four. Then we continued for another couple of hours before camping for the night. Without question, the hour before our one o'clock rest was the longest and hardest of the day. The sand would become too hot to walk on, forcing me to put on my shoes. The burning sand would then get between my toes, rubbing the skin, and my feet would start itching with friction and heat. The only thought that got me through that hour of discomfort was that it would be followed by a three-hour rest.

During the break, we would lie beneath a shelter, eating our snacks of dates and sweets, rehydrating, and perhaps sleeping a little. Mostly we talked. The team roamed through topics of conversation from the inane to the profound. We'd talk about differences in our cultures, our hobbies and interests, feminism, our routines back home, and how we

Watching the sun set over the Sugar Dunes

intended to make an impact in the world. We laughed a lot. I realized how little the team had been able to communicate with one another in Iceland. Now we had that opportunity for dialogue, and I felt like we all got much closer as a result.

Though I loved this camaraderie, my favorite moments were those I spent alone with the desert. In the evenings I would slip away from the camp and hide behind the dunes to watch the starry skies. I would wander far enough from the others to not be able to hear a sound or see any light. I sat for hours, alone, just gazing at the stars and thinking about my days and the exhilarating experience of stepping into the unknown, each step bringing us closer to the North Pole. I was sure that the process of adapting to a different wilderness and to each other

Lamees in the foreground relishing the heat of the Oman desert while Nataša, pictured in the background sitting on her sledge during a break, finds the environment a little more challenging

was going to make us each stronger, wiser, and more appreciative of our individual lives.

Returning to camp I almost always chose to sleep outside, taking care to place the mat and my sleeping bag right next to my team's tent so that I could talk to Susan and Steph at night through the tent fabric. I am a woman of the desert, and at first I couldn't understand why my tent-mates didn't feel the same and appeared so edgy.

"Did you feel this same way in Iceland, Lamees?" Steph asked me. "A feeling that you are completely out of your comfort zone and just want to go home?"

It was very strange to hear such words. What's to find uncomfortable? *I asked myself.* Being on a holiday in the desert for ten days? Enjoying the day and night breeze? Walking barefoot on soothing sand? How could this be annoying for anyone?

Admittedly, we did have to be careful to keep hydrated at all times, but I could sleep outside without worrying about freezing my flesh, I didn't have to be concerned about sweeping snow inside the tent on my clothing, and it did not take forever to prepare a hot drink. Compared to our experience in Iceland, it all felt joyous to me!

Sometimes my tent-mates would join me to gaze at the stars for a while, but every night I kept looking at the sky until I fell asleep. Some mornings I woke to the sound of a strong wind blowing and sending a majestic plume of sand blasting over my head. Most mornings I woke drenched in dew, but no matter what, every morning I felt blessed and thankful.

Nothing feels better than waking up in nature. Up before the rest of the team, I would find a perfect spot for my morning prayers. I'd watch the sun rise, waiting for the morning mist to evaporate while I sat quietly with morning coffee and cereal. The view of the sand dunes was phenomenal, and I'd relish this beautiful view without saying a word, enjoying the sound of silence. I'd try to decipher the marks left in the sand, which had been smooth and unblemished the night before but transformed each morning into a chaos of animal tracks. Was that sinuous indent the track of a snake moving on sand? Perhaps these trefoil patterns were a desert mouse with its tiny little cute steps? Here, I imagined a falcon had caught something and flown away, leaving a trail. It was one of the best ways to enjoy the first hour before the wind scoured the tracks. I learned a lot about the desert, the wind direction, the stars, the desert life.

During the final days of training we trekked through dunes close to the sea, so rich in salt that the sand was white. They were called the Sugar Dunes, and I had never before seen such pale sand. Its flour-like softness made it hard to walk, each footfall sinking deep. We tried to stick to the top of the dunes where progress was easier and from where we could spy the sea from a distance. A beautiful breeze blew toward

*us from the water and brought relief from the heat and the promise of
the end of our training. The sight made us sing, celebrating reaching
our destination. By the time we reached the beach we flung off our
harnesses and ran straight into the water, splashing each other, feeling
it on our body, and washing all the exhaustion away. We were laughing,
jumping, celebrating in every way and taking lots of pictures. It was
a happy moment, and I don't think I will ever forget the feeling of
finishing and how fresh we all felt in that sea.*

IDA: *In Oman I would sometimes take a solitary walk in the cool of the
evening. I would walk barefoot along the tops of the sand dunes, feeling*

The team on sand dunes in the Wahiba Sands desert of Oman

the breeze from the unseen ocean nearby. In every direction I was surrounded by mountains of sand so pale that I could be deceived into thinking I was in the Arctic or my home country of Sweden, surrounded by snow. It was the desert of my dreams.

We'd set up camp right before sunset, as we did each day of the expedition, and I would think how much easier it was to camp in the snow than in the desert. Snow can come into the tent just like sand and, yes, it is cold, but as long as you dress the right way it is all okay. True, there are polar bears in the Arctic, and you have to erect an alarmed trip-wire bear fence around the tent or have a polar bear guard who is awake all night. But there are no real monsters, not like those in the desert. We had to take great care about where we put our tent to avoid all the terrifying creatures that came out with the darkness: huge spiders, scorpions, and snakes. Once the tent is pitched you have to make sure the door zipper is closed as tightly as possible to avoid sharing the small space with anything other than your human tent-mates. I was always worried that something had crawled inside my sleeping bag.

Then there was the heat. I love to be outdoors in the sunshine, but the sunshine I relish feels soft and gentle. The heat of the desert is not soft at all; it's hard, searing, painful. I noticed at once how this heavy heat made me weak. I couldn't walk as fast as I was used to, and I wasn't as alert as usual. I am used to excelling in the extreme environment of the north, but in this opposite extreme I had to fight to keep my physical and mental energy at the levels I expected and needed—not just for my sake but so that I could maintain my role in providing good support for the rest of the team.

But I learned and adjusted. I observed the habits of my Arabic teammates, who were more familiar with the relentless heat of the desert. I wound a light scarf around my head as they did, but it didn't feel right. I've learned all my life to put on a hat to keep a warm body *temperature—to keep the heat in—and remove it only to ventilate. To cover my head in the desert was counterintuitive.*

Imitating Anisa and Lamees, I'd start the day walking barefoot and found I loved the feeling of the cool sand going between my toes. It felt so free, no double layers of woolen socks and no big heavy winter boots weighing down every step. But by midmorning the sand was too hot and the shoes would go back on. I would long for any breath of wind to cool the air. The wind made it all so much more pleasant and made it possible to enjoy the scenery, making every footstep feel easy. But often the wind never came, and the only respite from the heat would be the beads of sweat running down my face.

MARIAM: *I joined the team in Oman. I had just returned from Nevada, where I had attended the Burning Man Festival, a man-made temporary universe created once a year for a week, filled with art, music, dance, workshops, installations, talks, costumes, and more. Before it all ends and everyone goes home, people gather around the largest sculptures and watch them burn. The idea is to cherish the present moment because everything fades away. To immerse yourself in it and then let it go.*

Standing by a campfire in the Wahiba Sands of Oman on the first night of training felt like a continuation of that adventure. I've always been mesmerized by fire. It provides so much: warmth and light and the power to turn a strange place into a cozy shelter, a home. We sat around it, staring at it, mostly in silence, as we prepared ourselves mentally for the new adventure about to begin. This desert is our home now, I told myself. It felt ceremonial.

This time there were no skis. No poles. Shoes, or no shoes, it was up to us. No layers. Bare skin. Sunscreen. Hats. Scarves to keep our heads cool. Lots of water breaks. The weather hovered around 40°C—over 100°F. And yet here were many similarities with our glacier training.

Meeting the other wanderers of the Arabian desert

The Arctic is, after all, often referred to as a polar desert. Both have extreme weather conditions, and the landscape appears infinite.

Growing up in Saudi Arabia, I had been to the desert many times, but never like this. I was experiencing the desert in a whole new light as we walked for hours in the sun. One foot in front of the other, over and over again. A lot of the sand was soft and my feet sank in. I felt the weight of the sledge and the scorching heat, but even so, I preferred this over the cold. I definitely felt more in my element. As silent and harsh as the desert can be, it is alive with texture and patterns, lizards and beetles. The tiny, fast lizards are masters of camouflage and bury their bodies in the sand for protection.

At night, the clear, starry sky made the pain of the day fade away as I thought about how tiny we are in this great big world. The desert space helped me focus on being present. On being fully in my body, with a clear mind, moving slowly and steadily, watching every step of the ground beneath me as I moved in the line, following or leading my team, like a continuous living being. You breathe, you find a rhythm, you trust, you surrender, and you flow.

As we pulled sledges in the desert for eight hours a day, the Bedouins looked at us with confused faces. It must have been an odd sight to see. One afternoon, we came across a tent in the middle of the desert, a shop in the middle of nowhere. A Bedouin woman was running the show, selling handmade crafts and gasoline. "What are you doing here?" she asked me. I tried to explain that we were a group of women from different parts of the world, learning about each other's culture and training for a trip to the North Pole, where we'll be walking for hours and pulling sledges just like these. I don't think she understood all this, but she looked at me and said, "May Allah give you strength." I wished her the same. As we parted ways, I looked back at her. I felt like she was an extension of our team but on her own mission—a powerful woman taking care of business. Stay strong and keep going, her presence seemed to tell me. I thought that she must be a good omen.

MISBA: *Going from Iceland to Oman was like going from a freezer to an oven. In Iceland, the Middle Eastern women had suffered badly at temperatures around 0°C, but now it was their turn to smile as we Europeans melted at temperatures over 100°F. The North Pole might be far colder than the coldest temperature ever recorded in my native Manchester, but in Oman I faced temperatures equal to the hottest recorded in England in the past hundred years!*

To me, sand was what you found on the beach in Blackpool or in the children's sandbox. The Omani variety was nothing like that. I couldn't make up my mind whether I liked this fine powdery material that got everywhere. It was most annoying when it inevitably found its way into my shoes. I quickly determined that it was easier to walk barefoot. Stepping over cool sand in the early morning was beautifully therapeutic, though by midday the sand became unbearably hot to walk on.

Celebrations on reaching the sea

The desert is a place of contrasts, baked by day and chilled by night. Everything shimmered in the heat, and the sun seemed to suck every drop of moisture from my body. By evening the wind would pick up and fling sand into my throat and eyes. The wet wipe I used to clean my face would quickly absorb sand and feel more like an abrasive facial scrub. Yet despite the discomforts I liked the desert better than the cold. There was life there: beetles and lizards, even the huge, fearsome but harmless camel spiders held fascination. Fortunately, we didn't see any snakes, which would have diminished my liking of the place.

Some of the dunes were armored in thorny bushes, where the sand petered out into rocky plains. The desert proved to be very challenging terrain for sledges. The dunes were difficult to climb and descend with sledges, and it was particularly tricky to walk along the summit ridges, which often gave way, tipping our sledges onto their sides. But at least we could talk to each other while we sledged; in Iceland our faces had been permanently covered in layers of protective material, making conversation difficult. In Oman I got to know the other team members much better, particularly when we faced frightening moments.

One evening, when the sun had long since set and twinkling stars were shining above the barren landscape, we sat waiting for Felicity, who had driven to the nearest town in a support vehicle to fetch fresh water and additional food supplies. We had expected her to be back before dark, but now we gazed out over the endless sea of sand with our headlamps searching for any sign of the returning jeep. We decided to put up one of our tents, but determining where to place our camp for the night was not easy. We needed to make sure we were well away from the herds of wandering goats and camels that drifted across the desert at night.

The whole team huddled into just one tent, ten of us in one small space, occasionally sending someone outside to check for any sign of Felicity. It was getting late and I was hungry, but inside the tent we distracted ourselves by taking selfies, sharing what snacks we had left from the day, and giggling at the farcical situation we found ourselves in. On my turn to leave the tent and check for the vehicle, I spotted beams of light shining into the sky. I could see headlights bouncing across the sand dunes. Food time! I thought. But then the lights abruptly changed direction. I ran to the edge of the dune, waving my lamp directly toward the car in the distance. The lights had gone and I couldn't go any farther than the edge of the dune. I was worried I might fall off the edge of the wall of sand and struggle to get back up again to where we had pitched the tent. For a moment I stood helpless, glaring out into the dark, fear of being lost thumping in my chest. Then those parallel shafts of light lit up the side of the dune below me once again. The relief was instant. They had found us.

Back, left to right: Misba, Susan, Felicity (five months pregnant), Mariam, Ida; front, left to right: Anisa, Lamees, Steph, Nataša

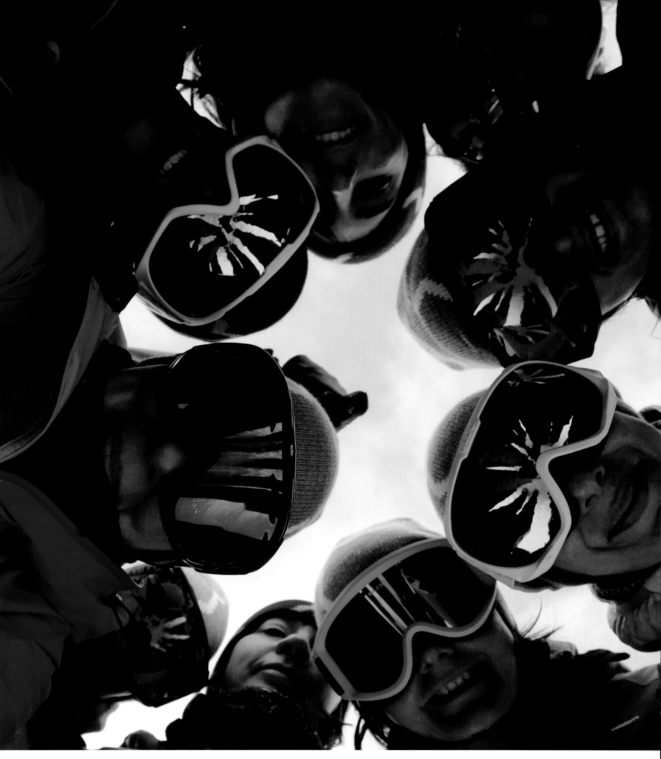

Clockwise from top: Asma, Mariam, Misba, Susan, Olga, Nataša, Felicity, Lamees

FIVE

Storm

Moving down the line of skiers making steady progress along a track of snow already compacted by snowmobiles, I fell in next to Asma, shortening my stride to match hers on our long cross-country skis. Pre-occupied with the organization of this second training expedition in Iceland, I hadn't managed to find an opportunity to speak to her much since our arrival in the country the night before.

Petite and always perfectly turned out, even when on expedition, I knew Asma as an exemplar of poise. Unfailingly courteous and good-humored, she never spoke without consideration and sensitive diplomacy. Quiet within the group, when she did speak, I had learned that it was always valuable to listen to what she had to say. I felt that I was continually learning from her.

As I got to know my Middle Eastern teammates better I became conscious that reputation and how they were perceived by others was important for them in a way that it had never been for me. I began to understand that they felt their actions and decisions could have consequences, not just for their standing in their society and for their futures but potentially for their families and associations too. I noticed how much more careful they were than their European counterparts about how they and their part in the expedition were presented to the world. They received resounding support but were also subject to intense scrutiny, particularly from within their own country. This must have added considerable pressure to their participation, and I felt it was the responsibility of the expedition to represent team members in the way that they wished.

Skiing alongside Asma through a snow-covered lava field in bright Icelandic sunshine, I listened as she spoke of her country, Qatar, and about her future ambitions. "In my country," she explained, "to call someone adventurous is to imply somehow that they are badly raised or reckless." Through her role at the Qatar Olympic Committee and now her experiences as part of the expedition, Asma had firsthand knowledge of the benefit sport and adventure can bring, both in terms of personal development and to the wider community. Her personal mission was to try and rehabilitate the meaning in Qatar of adventure and of being an adventurous person—and to do that by transforming herself into the role model she felt her country needed.

I felt goose bumps rise on my skin. Asma's voice was measured, but I heard determination and strength in her words. This was a woman who would do great things, I felt sure of it.

It was almost a year since we had departed Oman at the end of our training expedition, and I had been working hard to ensure that our wished-for opportunity to ski to the North Pole would become real. We had a strong and committed expedition team, with credibility earned in training. We had a story that could inspire, empower, and do some good in working toward positive change. Now all we needed was the financial support to enable us to put our careful plans into action. Traveling to the North Pole is an expensive proposition—as it should be, the logistics and expertise required are vast—but finding the funds is daunting.

During my polar career, I've been fortunate to enjoy the support of many wonderful organizations that have enabled me to realize fantastic dreams—but none more so than the cybersecurity firm Kaspersky Lab. In 2009, they sponsored the international women's team I led to the South Pole, and in 2012 they sponsored my solo ski across Antarctica. I was overjoyed when they said they would continue that support for this new endeavor.

The timing was serendipitous. Kaspersky Lab had recently published a report they had commissioned that investigated the lack of women in senior roles within the cybersecurity industry. One of the report's key findings was the importance of visible female role models to encourage more women to aspire to those senior positions. As a result, Kaspersky Lab had committed to supporting female role models not just within their own industry but beyond it too. Though the expedition was not in the business of cybersecurity, it did create visible female role models and would inspire women to reach for greater aspirations. Kaspersky Lab saw value in partnering with the expedition to amplify our story and to make sure it succeeded.

Kaspersky Lab also introduced me to Olga, a mountaineer they had sponsored to climb the highest volcano on every continent—a project that had taken Olga to Antarctica and the most remote reaches of South America and Asia. She had experience of expedition life and extreme environments, so I was confident she would be able to fit into the expedition at such a late stage, but with just a couple of months to go until we departed for the Arctic Ocean, I was aware that it would be a tough ask for both her and the team.

OLGA: *When I was a child in the USSR, books and films about expeditions to the Arctic and the North Pole were very popular. We grew up playing at being polar explorers and dreaming that one day we would make an expedition to the Arctic. It was not realistic; we were not supposed to dream about other countries. Foreign lands were out of reach, only accessible through television shows. When you live in such*

The team on skis ready to depart on the second training expedition in Iceland, reflected in the goggles of a teammate

an environment you stop noticing it as anything to question and it just becomes normality. We accepted things as they were.

It may sound strange coming from someone who grew up in northern Russia and has been obsessed with the North Pole a long time, but I have to confess that I don't like the cold. Usually I spend winters somewhere warm. My hands are the biggest problem; they're always cold. The first thing I did after accepting a place on the expedition was to buy several pairs of the warmest mittens I could find. The thought of skiing across windswept Arctic ice haunted my dreams. But I kept telling myself that this was my only way to the pole.

I was joining the team late. The rest of the group had been together for more than a year and had already completed two full training expeditions together. As I traveled to Iceland for the team's third and final training, the thought of joining an already established group worried me. I am acutely aware that I am an introvert. Despite having worked as a travel guide for a decade, with a lot of time spent with strangers, I've never quite lost the discomfort it brings me. I don't mesh well with people easily and dislike large groups. So the thought of living so closely with ten women from different countries on this expedition made me anxious. For years I had either undertaken solo expeditions or been the leader and organizer of an expedition. I struggled to remember what it was like to be a member of a team. Following was a new role for me, and I wasn't sure if I could find the right balance. But I had made my choice and had to overcome my hang-ups if I wanted the ultimate reward of making it to the top of the world.

I had braced myself for the worst and discovered on arrival that my anxieties had been well founded. Due to bad weather, everything had been delayed, so rather than arriving with a few days to meet everyone and prepare for heading out into the blustery Icelandic highlands, we had to start training immediately. Everything was a rush. When I arrived at the meeting place it was already dark. There was a lot of activity, everyone running around, everyone busy. The team greeted me in a jumble of names and faces but immediately returned to their tasks. I was unclear where to go or what to do. I had to forget about relaxed introductions. My inner introvert demanded a gradual easing into the teamwork, and I felt stressed. My tent-mate Steph came over and began *explaining to me what was going on. Her words tumbled out rapid-fire, and not for a moment did she stop working on her tasks. In this bustle I forgot how to speak English and became overwhelmed. The only thing I understood was that we had to load our sledges and skis and leave. My head was spinning.* As Steph continued talking, I said to myself, This is a complete failure.

Fortunately it was decided we should get some sleep before our departure early the next morning, and we all dispersed to our own rooms. That was great for me. It's not that I didn't want to see anyone; it was just that I needed time to absorb what was happening. By the next morning I was ready. I understood everything I was told. The team members seemed like my old companions, and I was glad I had taken the time to memorize everyone's names based on their pictures. I was particularly glad to see Nataša. I had met her in Oslo Airport while we waited for the same plane to Iceland. I had been embarrassed because she had caught me eating a sugary pastry with my coffee. I had assumed that in an all-female team there would be a lot of talk about healthy eating. But then I had noticed the greasy hamburger she was eating. She immediately began telling me that we had to eat up prior to our adventure in the cold. I was relieved.

We set out early the next day. At first, everything was easy—but then Iceland greeted us with a hurricane. In the middle of our first night the winds tried hard to break our tents, and we spent all the next day battling the furious Icelandic weather, constantly having to dig our shelter out of the snow and trying to keep it from collapsing. If this is just a training session, I thought, what can we expect at the pole? *For hours that day we were cooped up inside the tent. From time to time someone had to crawl outside and dig away the accumulated snow so that the tent would not collapse under its weight. The snow was forever bearing down and inward, leaving less and less space for us inside.*

Since I had the shovel (and the most experience with snowstorms), I

The rush to get the team ready to leave our overnight accommodation in the remote highlands of Iceland and out into the wild before the storm hit

crawled outside repeatedly to excavate the snow. The wind was blowing harder and harder and the snow was building up ever faster. Once, as I was getting ready to go outside, Lamees offered to go with me. I was taken aback because this fragile-looking Kuwaiti had only ever seen snow once before, and that had been during the previous training expedition in Iceland. Out of everyone in the tent, her offer to help was the least expected. But her help was very timely. Working together we shoveled the snow twice as fast.

That night, as we settled in and the storm continued, I reflected on how this expedition was going to be different from any previous trip

I had been a part of. What particularly struck me was the need for order and discipline within the team. My previous expeditions had not needed strict roles for each team member or extensive training for all contingencies. There had been room for more flexibility and initiative from the team members (admittedly, not always with good results). But for this expedition, in the harsh environment of the North Pole and with a large number of team members with minimal polar experience, I could see that the order and discipline were essential.

I was also surprised to find that I enjoyed spending this time with my tent-mates: Steph, Susan, and Lamees. I enjoyed being a part of this group of ten very different but very capable women, all working together to achieve something glorious. I was impressed and inspired by the team's eagerness to learn and train in the most extreme conditions. I wasn't going to lose my introvert nature overnight, but I did feel my pretrip anxieties, one by one, being addressed and fading. After meeting the team members and learning how the expedition was being organized and prepared for, I had no doubt that our team was ready and prepared to reach the North Pole. I was also sure that I would reach it alongside them.

STEPH: *I was worried when, ahead of our last training session in Iceland, Felicity told us our tent would be joined by a new team member, Olga, from Russia. Susan, Lamees, and I had created a tight team that worked brilliantly together. The humor between us came easily, and through gentle teasing of each other we had built a strong sense of camaraderie. Lamees was the youngest and took on a role of little sister in our tent team. Slim and athletic, she was constantly brushing the fringe of her shoulder-length dark brown hair away from her eyes. It was clear that she was in her element being out in nature under the stars and was determined to soak in every second of the experience.*

Susan had a soft French accent that was instantly comforting. She was svelte and strong, exuding a calm confidence that invited trust. She was a great foil to my more boisterous manner. I felt lucky to have two tent-mates I could count on to muck in when necessary, and we had begun referring to ourselves as the "Three Musketeers." It was a bond that would only deepen.

I didn't want anything to disrupt our happy tent harmony, and I worried Olga's addition might disrupt the precious bubble of trust that was so important to me and which I knew would be so vital on the ice. Her experience worried me. She had worked as a mountain

From left: Susan, Lamees, and Steph, who shared a tent and got on so well that they came to refer to themselves as the "Three Musketeers"

guide, traveling to many extreme places around the world, so I doubted whether she would be able to adapt to being told what to do or have much interest in fitting into the team routines we'd already established.

I decided to assign Olga to outdoor duties, which would mean spending time with me outside the tent securing the tent and sledges each evening. I have particular expectations and standards about securing a tent properly, so I prefer to do it myself. However, I felt I could more easily adjust my routine to accommodate a new person rather than disrupt the partnership Lamees and Susan had developed for the jobs inside the tent.

Steph in her tent, almost overwhelmed by the sheer volume of clothing and equipment. Being well organized was essential.

We made a conscious effort to be sociable in the tent and put Olga at ease. Her English was hesitant, but Lamees was particularly interested in hearing about her adventures, and Olga grew really animated as she described the exotic places she'd visited. But during our very first evening together, while working outside the tent, Olga got frustrated when I suggested for the third time that we should make sure all the poles and guy ropes securing the tent were well anchored. She responded that the weather was mild, pointing to the sky.

"What if the weather changes overnight?" I asked.

Olga stared at me for a moment, and I imagined she thought me paranoid. With a slight shrug of the shoulders and a dismissive shake of the head, she started to shovel snow onto the ropes that secured our tent to the ground.

That night I woke with a jolt. The tent was flapping wildly. I checked my watch. It was one-thirty and no one else was awake. I closed my eyes but knew I wouldn't be able to rest again until the wind died down. Staring at the flapping roof, I thought about Misba and Asma, who were in a tent by themselves. I hoped they had built up enough snow around their tent to protect them from the wind for the night. At least our tent had the weight of four bodies to stop it from taking off. I tugged my bobble hat down to cover my ears, hoping I could block out the sound for a little longer, knowing that it was bound to get worse before it got better.

I drifted in and out of nervous sleep, and by dawn the flapping was even more vicious. By eight everyone was awake. It was impossible to sleep through the wind now, even with earplugs. None of us had moved, however, and we were still hidden within the warmth of our sleeping bags, staring at the sides of the tent. I'd experienced a storm like this before, during the expedition to Antarctica with Felicity, and knew how this could end. I wondered if my tent-mates were as concerned as I was. I felt hugely vindicated that our tent was upright and still withstanding the wind, though I didn't say anything to Olga.

By ten the gale-force wind was smashing into the tent from all directions so furiously that we had to shout at each other just to make ourselves heard. Suddenly, Felicity's voice rose over the noise. "Get out of the tent. Get out of the tent. A tent has collapsed!" she shouted.

Susan and Olga, with an efficiency that would come to define them, were dressed in no time, checking each other's face to ensure they were both completely covered, pulling on their boots, and heading out into the storm. Lamees followed, forgetting to zip the door up behind her. The wind howled straight through the tent opening and froze my uncovered face. I grabbed my ski boots only to find that the laces had frozen solid, then pulled out my jacket and found that the zip on that had frozen too.

Felicity's fleece-smothered head suddenly appeared in the tent doorway. "Come on, Steph. We need you. Get out here," she shouted over the roar of windblown tent fabric.

In a panic, I decided to head out—to hell with my frozen gear. I pulled my neck gaiter over my nose, hastily placed my goggles over my eyes, flung on my down jacket, and walked out into the storm, stomping as hard as possible in the hope that my feet would eventually slide into my boots, which had frozen out of shape. I could barely see through the swirling snow, but I could just make out a misshapen tent, one half flattened and writhing in the wind. Three figures had created a human chain, hurriedly passing on to safety the contents from inside the collapsed tent. Two other figures were rescuing expedition equipment buried under the snow, while another was busy piling shovel-loads onto the collapsed part of the tent in a bid to keep it from getting damaged further by the wind. It was Asma and Misba's tent. I couldn't see them, and on my way over to help, Felicity stopped me. "Make sure your tent isn't going anywhere," she shouted before rushing off to her own tent to do the same.

Even though I had been out of the tent for seconds, I was covered in snow and my thermal layer was soaked. My bulky, heavily insulated down jacket looked damp and useless. I shoveled more snow onto the walls around our tent to reinforce them and dug snow away in places where dangerously large and heavy drifts had built up too close, their weight bearing down on the sides of the tent. Felicity was suddenly next to me, double-checking the state of our tent. I shouted out to her. "This all feels very familiar!"

"Doesn't it just," she replied, sounding exhausted.

I knew she must have been having the same flashbacks as I was, to the storm we had experienced together in Antarctica and which had also destroyed our tents.

Fighting their way back to the tent against the wind, Susan and Lamees looked pale with the shock of experiencing the true force of nature for the first time and realizing how vulnerable we were. I wanted to point out that this was without the temperatures we'd be facing at the pole, but I didn't say anything.

Back inside the tent no one said a word as I peeled off my wet clothes and positioned my back against one of the poles keeping the sides of the tent rigid, still wearing my damp thermal underwear and no socks. Susan joined me on Olga's side of the tent, positioning herself against another pole while the other two lay in the middle of the tent. Our backs took a beating as the wind pummeled the fabric, but we were keeping the tent upright by providing resistance.

Time passed by excruciatingly slowly. There's not much to do in a storm when you're stuck in a tent except eat and sleep. Lamees reminded us of the deck of cards that, in our eagerness to pack as lightweight as possible, we had made her leave behind. I groaned with regret. Boredom is a nasty affliction. At one point Olga noticed that the snow was piling up into a drift, putting more pressure on one side of the tent and offered to go outside to clear it.

Although Olga was the oldest in our tent, she was as strong as an ox. She didn't need help to dig away a little snow, but Lamees jumped at *the chance to head out into the storm. I understood. I probably would have gone too if I'd had any dry clothes, just to break the monotony of the hours inside. In the end, Olga and Lamees shoveled snow from around the tent another three times that day, as the storm refused to calm. During the long moments of silence I contemplated the scenarios of both remaining tents collapsing and having to be outside in wet gear. I wondered if it was cold enough to get frostbite or hypothermia. I imagined what this storm would have been like at the North Pole, where my gear wouldn't dry.*

From left: Lamees, Olga, and Asma in Iceland during the second training expedition. Note how the poles of the tent in the background are all bent out of shape because of the storm the day before.

I also wondered what my teammates were thinking. A storm like this can destroy confidence just as it destroys tents. Doubts started to emerge and the reality of what we were each laying on the line was very clear. These places can kill you no matter how many modern satellite gismos and fancy jackets you have. The bottom line was that our success—no, our survival—rested on our ability to coexist with the weather and to endure, not just as individuals but, most importantly, as a group.

It was uncomfortable to realize how reliant I was on near-strangers for my very well-being. Suddenly, whether someone snores or laughs at your jokes or talks too much becomes less important than whether they can keep their gear dry, whether they remember to zip up the tent each time they go outside, whether they can be trusted not to cut corners on the vital details like properly securing tent ropes or building a decent snow wall against the wind. Details matter. As we sat in silence listening to the wind all day, I hoped the same message was sinking into the minds of my teammates.

MISBA: *I was excited to be returning to Iceland. The country had always felt mysterious to me. It was somewhere my children had come on school trips and returned with talk of active volcanoes, powerful waterfalls, and erupting geysers. I hadn't been able to imagine such a place. Now, arriving for my second visit, I was quickly dealing with my first disappointment. Of my tent group of four, neither Ida nor Anisa was able to join this last training expedition, which left just Asma and me in our tent.*

Being without our tent-mates was particularly difficult when a 100-mile-an-hour windstorm tore across our fragile shelter. We both lay across the floor of the tent desperately trying to keep it stable. The wind was flattening the tent in one direction while snow was piling up against the opposite wall, making the tent lopsided as the weight of the amassed snow threatened to crush us inside. It was bitterly cold, and it had been hours since I had been able to light the stove and make any food or hot water for drinks.

Asma's head was bouncing like a woodpecker as the wind battered the flimsy material of the tent wall. She was worried that we were being trapped inside by the buildup of snow. To reassure her that we could still get out, I unzipped the door—only to find it completely blocked. Aghast, Asma fished her phone from her pocket where she kept it warm and frantically started sending email messages to the team asking for help. The other tents were less than a few strides away, yet due to the storm they might as well have been on the moon. A particularly ferocious gust of wind made the tent lurch to one side, leaving us crouching inside like babies in the womb. I was aware that now the only thing keeping the tent on the ground was our body weight—and neither Asma nor I are what you would call bulky.

"No one is replying to my emails," Asma said, "I am going to get out."

"No, don't. You'll get blown away, the wind is so fierce."

The noise of the wind was so ferocious it gave me a headache. My socks were wet where they had been in contact with the tent wall as I tried to hold back the weight of the snow, so I removed them and put dry gloves on my feet instead.

Suddenly, without a word, Asma left her position propping up the tent and slipped out into the storm through the doorway, leaving it open behind her. I called after her before realizing that she wouldn't hear me over the tremendous noise of the wind. She had left without her shoes, even, going out into the snow in just her socks. Without her weight propping up the shelter, half the tent immediately collapsed. Alarmed, I started digging out my boots and in an awkward crouched position struggled to get them on my wet feet.

I waited for Asma to return with help, but no one came. I worried she hadn't made it to our neighboring tents and that the rest of the *team would be oblivious. In a panic I started to stuff my sleeping bag into a black bin liner in an attempt to keep it dry. My wet toes and bare fingers started to feel dangerously numb and I wished I had put on socks and gloves first. With a rush of snow rolling heavily onto the tent, it finally collapsed completely.*

Then I heard voices. Finally, help was here.

NATAŠA: *I was procrastinating. I checked my sleeping bag again, then a third time, making sure it was correctly positioned and half opened in just the right way so that I could get in as fast as I could upon returning to it. I reminded myself where I would put my wet underwear and where I would find the dry set of clothes I had prepared. Mariam was making tea at the far end of the tent, anticipating that I would need warming up with a hot drink when I returned all soaking wet and freezing.*

"You can do it," she called out in encouragement. I knew I had it under control, but still I was grateful for her comment. We'd already made it through a hurricane on this trip. Surely this experience couldn't be any worse.

The "ice-breaking" drill, as Felicity called it, involved deliberately submerging ourselves in a stream of supercold water. The idea was to ensure that we would know what to do if the sea ice at the North Pole were to break underfoot as we skied across it, sending us into the icy ocean beneath. I was terrified at the thought. I really do not like cold water. I avoid washing my hands in it, much less swimming in it. I recognized, however, that immersion was a scenario, no matter how unlikely, that could happen on our journey over the Arctic Ocean and that I would be foolish to avoid proper training for this horrible eventuality. I needed to feel how my body would respond when exposed to freezing water.

When Felicity had first mentioned the ice-breaking drill, I expected that we would simply go through the theory of it, talk hypothetically about what to do if anyone fell into the water. Then I found out what we were really doing. So there I was, in front of the freezing stream of glacial meltwater, in subzero temperatures and up to my ankles in snow. I would regret not having this experience, I told myself. I knew I couldn't skip this part of the training but was happy that there was no one to take a photo of my face. Suddenly I was struck by the ridiculousness of the situation—women from all over the world standing in our underwear in the middle of the snowy Icelandic wilderness waiting to throw ourselves into cold water, ready to obediently follow any instructions to do such a ridiculous thing. What were we thinking?

I felt the cold on my feet as I walked in my socks through the snow to reach Felicity. "Go. Go, go, jump in and turn around," she called. It seemed to me that those in front of me had done their job with ease. I envied the women who had already completed the drill. I was worried I might scream just before I had to throw myself into the water. Then I remembered that a few years before, while traveling around Brittany, I had braved a New Year's Eve swim and bathed in water colder than 10°C (50°F). So in theory I had some idea of what to expect.

My turn came. The water in the stream rose barely to my knees. I looked up to the sky and with clenched teeth I lay down in the water. Somewhere in the distance I heard Felicity call, "You're doing great. Way to go, bravo Nataša!" I felt relief that I hadn't been hit by any demons at the last minute. I hadn't screamed.

"And now the procedure of getting out of the water," Felicity said, and I awkwardly twirled my legs and arms to grab ski poles and simulated how I would make it onto the ice if I had really fallen into the water of the Arctic Ocean. I maneuvered the ski poles as if I was doing some old tribal dance, then rolled about in the snow (which we were told would soak up any excess water from our clothes). The whole scene must have looked quite absurd.

The speed with which I returned to the preheated tent from the drill was my most impressive feat. I was shivering but glowing with relief that it was over. I scolded myself for making a fuss as I threw on dry clothes and sank my feet deep into the warmed sleeping bag waiting for me.

Now it was Olga's turn. We had only known Olga for a few days, but it was already clear that she was one tough lady. As she left the tent for her turn at the drill she gave the impression she was taking a stroll on a sunny beach somewhere. I couldn't detect any emotion. Mariam and I stared in amazement. Exchanging glances, we both just said, "Wow." I was left wishing I could have managed to look so composed. When Olga returned to the tent she shared with Steph, Lamees, and Susan, it was again as if nothing had happened. As she unhurriedly stripped off her wet clothes I asked her, "Are you cold, Olga? Do you need anything?" She replied casually: "I'm fine, I'm fine. Don't worry." I glanced again at Mariam, who was still open-mouthed in amazement. We were both impressed and perhaps just a little intimidated by such a display of mental strength.

The team on the iced beach close to Longyearbyen, testing newly allocated equipment and watched by a BBC news crew

SIX

Longyearbyen

The paw-shaped islands of Svalbard lying due north of Norway constitute almost the last scrap of solid ground before you reach the North Pole. The islands and the main settlement, Longyearbyen, have long been used as a staging post for those exploring the northernmost reaches of the Arctic and seeking the top of the world.

The history of Arctic exploration is one littered with stories of horrific, lingering ways to die on sea ice. Foremost amongst them is the "lost" expedition of Sir John Franklin, which was sent north in 1845 by the British Admiralty to discover the Northwest Passage, a long-hoped-for shipping route connecting the Atlantic to the Pacific via the icy waters north of the American continent. They never returned, leaving a public desperate to know their fate. Over the next 150 years, dozens of expeditions tracked the Franklin expedition into the Arctic and eventually pieced together evidence of a gruesome story. Having found themselves trapped in sea ice, stranded in a wilderness they did not understand and were ill-equipped to endure, the Franklin expedition spent two winters confined to their ships before trying to flee for the mainland over the frozen sea. None survived. The remains and artifacts that were discovered record slow, agonizing deaths variously caused by hypothermia, starvation, poisoning, scurvy, and other inevitable nutritional deficiencies, as well as disease, accident, and violence. Most disturbing of all were the signs of cannibalism among the last to die, a telling insight into the depths of desperation these men must have reached by the end as they died on the ice.

It is a morbid irony that many more than the 129 men lost on the Franklin expedition died during the expeditions sent by both land and by sea to find them. Greater numbers still perished in the golden age of Arctic exploration that followed, most succumbing during grueling ordeals across the sea ice. In 1879, the US Arctic Expedition on the USS *Jeannette* spent two years trapped in drifting ice off northeast Siberia before being crushed and sunk, marooning her thirty-three crew on the ice. Dragging lifeboats and provisions over rough floes, the party discovered after their first week of punishing travel toward dry land that the drift of the pack ice had actually moved them farther away from their goal than when they had started. Only thirteen men made it back alive. In 1912 a Russian exploration ship, the *Saint Anna*, with thirty-three crew (including a female nurse) spent over a year trapped in pack ice before thirteen of the crew decided to try to escape across the frozen sea. Two of this party were the only survivors of the expedition, each leaving a detailed and harrowing account of their 90-day, 235-mile ordeal on pack ice to reach safety.

Ships trapped in ice followed by fraught and often fatal journeys in dismal pursuit of survival became a frequent, almost expected, pattern of Arctic exploration. In some cases, the entrapment was relied on. Norwegian explorer Fridtjof Nansen commissioned the *Fram*, a ship designed specifically to be deliberately frozen into the northern pack ice. His revolutionary hypothesis was that the drift of the ice over the ocean would carry the ship with it to the North Pole. In March 1895, after eighteen months of erratic movement with currents and storms across the Arctic Ocean, the ship had reached a latitude of 84 degrees north. Impatient, Nansen left the *Fram* with a companion to dogsled over the sea ice, heading for the pole—a staggering decision given what was known at that time about the hazards of travel over the frozen sea.

After three weeks, Nansen and his companion, Johansen, were farther north than anyone had ever been but still some 250 miles from the North Pole. Worse, Nansen realized they were battling a dramatic southward drift. The pair made the decision to turn around and set out on what is one of the most astonishing journeys over sea ice ever undertaken. They set course for Franz Josef Land, a remote archipelago even by the standards of the high Arctic, which had been discovered just twenty years earlier. As pack ice transformed into fragmented floes and eventually ice-filled waters, Nansen and Johansen gradually killed their dogs and adapted their equipment to the changing environment, turning sledges into kayaks and hunting for food. After four months on the ice they finally set foot on rock but spent a frugal winter camped on an island before preparing for another monumental journey over the new year's ice to Svalbard, where rescue was more hopeful. Miraculously they were spared this last epic, stumbling across a British expedition that was able to relieve them.

Even the advent of air flight at the end of the nineteenth century couldn't completely protect explorers from the hazards of Arctic sea ice. As the *Fram* headed home to Norway in 1896, it stopped briefly in Svalbard, where the courageous, if arguably foolhardy, Swedish aeronaut Salomon Andrée was preparing to fly over the Arctic Ocean with two companions in a hot air balloon. The following year they crashed onto the pack after two days of flying, forcing a three-month trek over ice toward Kvitøya, a small islet on the outer reaches of Svalbard. Within a few days of coming ashore all three men had died.

Sea ice continues to be deadly to the present day. In 2015, an experienced Dutch polar explorer, Marc Cornelissen, went missing with his traveling companion, scientist Philip de Roo, during a research expedition on skis from Resolute Bay to Bathurst Island in the Canadian

Arctic. Cornelissen's body was later recovered, along with a husky that had been traveling with the team to guard against polar bears. The husky was found still alive and loyally protecting Cornelissen's half-unpacked sledge on an ice floe. A second sledge was found in the

Sea ice is aesthetically beautiful, but history tells us it is also reliably lethal.

water nearby. It is speculated that Cornelissen died of hypothermia after trying to rescue de Roo when he fell into the water through thin or unstable ice.

This tragic litany of lives lost was a constant, grim reminder of the hazards of the journey ahead of my team of unlikely polar novices. The responsibility I felt to ensure that they were as prepared and as

well-equipped as any expedition setting out to the North Pole deepened as we drew closer to our departure date. Leaving Iceland at the end of our last training expedition, we had just six weeks before we were due to head to Svalbard, where we would wait for a flight to the Arctic Ocean. Stitching together all the logistical elements to make sure team, equipment, support, and outreach were exactly where they needed to be at exactly the right time was a task of Herculean proportions. I began to notice a brittleness in myself as the relentless pressures of managing such a sprawling, evolving, multifaceted expedition mounted. The consequences of getting anything wrong—in terms of safety, success, and funding—were acute. Just as I was beginning to imagine we were successfully through the worst of it, I received a late-night email informing me (and everyone else hoping to fly to the Arctic Ocean that season) that due to a bureaucratic issue the season might be canceled—or at least delayed—by anything from a few days to a couple of weeks. With people and their equipment poised at airports around the world waiting to hear whether or not they should get on a plane, I wrestled with impossible decisions, weighing up the merits of innumerable possibilities. It was a high-stakes logistical puzzle, one made more complex by the addition of a full-blown film production.

American filmmaker Holly Morris had originally applied to be part of the expedition team. There wasn't the capacity within the project to add a representative from the United States, but Holly's description of herself on the application form as a "dog with a bone" proved to be no exaggeration. Refusing to give up, she proposed making a film of the expedition instead. At first I wasn't enthusiastic. The expedition couldn't afford to pay for a film, and in working on film production expeditions in the past I had seen the difficulty of combining both filming objectives and expedition goals; one or the other ended up being sacrificed. Undeterred, Holly sent me a copy of her most recent film and promised that she would source the funding for the film production herself.

Holly's previous work focused largely on stories of women whose experiences had given them an interesting and uncommon perception of the world, allowing her subjects the space and respect they deserved to share their reality. One of the central goals of our expedition was to engage an audience in the issues that we as a team would explore, and I began to see that a film, done in the right way, could capture those insights and reach a far broader audience than we could manage through press and social media alone. Holly's plan was to form a production team that would accompany the expedition on all its training journeys, visit team members in their own homes, and ski to the North Pole with us. The production would become part of the fabric of the expedition while simultaneously remaining a completely separate and independent entity. We decided that, during the ski to the North Pole, Holly and two camera operators would be joined by two professional polar guides to form an "expedition within the expedition." Though aligned to the team, the film crew would remain self-sufficient and autonomous, the guides looking after the film crew's safety and hauling the bulk of the camera equipment, which would allow the camera operators the freedom to move and film deftly.

The plan asked a lot of the guides, so I was hugely reassured when two very experienced Arctic guides agreed to take it on. Caroline Hamilton had led both the first British women's team to ski to the South Pole and the first women's team to ski to the North Pole. Ann Daniels had been on both those teams and had since become a much-respected Arctic guide as well as making one of very few attempts by a woman to ski solo to the North Pole (a feat still yet to be achieved). With Ann and Caroline as their guides, Holly and her film crew would be in expert hands. I had met Ann and Caroline many years before as I prepared to take part in one of my very first Arctic journeys. We'd met in a central London bar called Champagne Charlie's, and as memorable as the advice they shared was the sense of fun and joy they had in what they did. They demonstrated that polar exploring didn't have to exclude fun, and to be a serious polar explorer you didn't have to walk around looking as glum as Amundsen.

Ann, Holly, and I finally had an opportunity to sit down together shortly before the expedition and reconfirm the plan—the film production would generally shadow the expedition team at a modest distance, allowing the team to forge our own route and progress over the ice exactly as if we were alone. Thrilled as I was to have the opportunity to travel with some of my polar heroes, by maintaining a clear separation between the expedition and the film teams we *were* on an expedition together and at the same time we *weren't*. I regretted that lack of interaction (and still do). It created an odd dynamic, and I came to resent the film production to some extent for being the cause of that barrier between us.

"We are the last thing you need," Caroline told me when we met in Svalbard. At first I didn't understand what she meant, but then I realized that having Ann and Caroline on the expedition felt like I was taking a driving test. I couldn't escape the feeling that I was going to be judged—and my heroes would be doing the judging. I tried hard to rid myself of the feeling. *Have faith in yourself,* I thought. I remembered all those times in the past when I had buckled under self-doubt only to wish afterward that I'd had more confidence in myself. This was the occasion to remember that lesson. *Ann and Caroline were professionals there to do a job, not to judge me,* I told myself. I was sure that they would be nothing but supportive.

Besides, my focus was needed on a dozen other matters. As team members arrived in Longyearbyen in clusters, and as the departure date for the ice continued to be unclear, I scrambled to find accommodation for everyone, to delegate tasks (both to reduce my workload and to keep anxious team members busy), and to deal with the daily onslaught of setbacks. At the last minute our insurance providers informed us of an oversight on their part that invalidated our medical evacuation and search-and-rescue insurance cover. Finding insurance for such an inherently risky undertaking had been nearly impossible in the first place, and now I faced starting the process from scratch, spending hours hunched over a telephone in our cramped rented accommodation, listening to music as I was put on hold through endless hotlines.

Stress comes with the territory of organizing an ambitious expedition to a challenging part of the world, but I worried about the impact it would have on the confidence of my teammates. I could sense the tension building as we faced yet more delays. I began to feel like a sailor desperately trying to plug the holes in a leaking ship as I tried to calm the nerves of an increasingly anxious team. I pleaded with the universe for our expedition to start…before my ship started to fall apart.

SUSAN: *Longyearbyen is a strange town. Open to the mountainous Arctic scenery that surrounds it, it is enclosed by rules that ban anyone from walking beyond the town perimeter because of the risk of polar bear encounters. Freedom and restriction simultaneously. For safety, none of the doors in the settlement was locked—you never knew when you might meet a bear that had strolled into town and need to seek the safety of a building. In a regular city you might see signs in banks and airports banning cameras or phones, but in Longyearbyen there were signs banning firearms. Strangest of all, there were no permanent residents. No one is allowed to be born or to die there. Instead the population drifts in and out, the tourists arriving with the light of spring and leaving only the most essential key workers to spend the dark Arctic winters there. It feels surreal and oddly disorienting.*

We were supposed to spend five days in Longyearbyen before our departure for the ice and the start of our expedition to the North Pole, but we stayed more than two weeks. Every day we congregated from our various accommodations, spread across that weird little town, to meet in the cozy coffee shop that had become our de facto headquarters. Felicity would go through the long list of things that needed to be done each day, and we would each report on our progress. Usually there was a new change of plan, a fresh delay, an additional challenge: a missing piece of equipment, running out of accommodation as departure was postponed, travel insurance for the North Pole falling through….

We were delegated tasks or split into groups to investigate solutions before wandering the icy roads of Longyearbyen to secure fuel containers for our sledges, pick up our jackets from the seamstress who had made last-minute adjustments, take part in interviews, or find a quiet spot to record a podcast with Nataša. We quickly became familiar with the streets and the shops. I even squeezed in a visit to a museum dedicated to Arctic explorers. It failed to mention any women.

As the days passed, I began to wonder if the expedition would happen at all. It felt like our chances of reaching the North Pole were thinning as fast as the ice we needed to ski over. The longer we stayed in Longyearbyen, the more anxious we became, driven not just by fear that the whole trip might be canceled but because the delay was allowing doubts to creep in about our abilities, both personally and as a team.

The town was full of famous and experienced Arctic guides who had gathered there to lead their own expeditions to the North Pole. You could tell who they were because they looked conspicuously at home and behaved as if the town belonged to them. They knew exactly where to go, never looking around to find their way. They knew where to hang their jackets when walking into a bar or restaurant and always seemed relaxed. And they just looked different. Not only because of their tanned faces and laid-back attitude but in their dress. We, the North Pole novices, wore new, shiny outdoor clothes, but the guides had a favorite hat, or knitted sweater, or patched-up jacket that they must have worn so many times—items of clothing that carried memories of past trips. Clothes that said, "You can trust me."

These guides fit precisely my mental image of a polar explorer. They had skied to the North Pole more times than they could remember, and they made no secret of their concern over the size of our group. They told us we were too many to be able to move quickly through the densely packed ice rubble, created when floes crashed together. If we needed to get through in a hurry, they told us, we would be backed up like a traffic jam. We started to see ourselves through their eyes and it was scary. We looked like a group of naive dreamers, some too young and some too old, all of us tired and worried and frantic.

One afternoon, Felicity gathered us to go to a warehouse to collect our skis for the expedition. Before we arrived she stopped us for a team talk to warn us that we would be meeting the people who ran the operation that would take us out onto the sea ice. "If they become concerned that we are not prepared or might not be capable of safely looking after ourselves out on the ice," she said, "they are perfectly within their right to refuse to take us." She asked us to be conscious of the impression we were making and to present our most professional selves. No giggling, no messing around.

We were all on our best behavior, but it wasn't easy. Humor was our way of diminishing our fear and bonding as a group. When we arrived, the warehouse was busy with stone-faced guides and polar geeks intently inspecting their gear. We were shown the collection from which we could select our skis and poles for our journey to the pole. We were all scared we'd be issued an inappropriate pair of skis or uncomfortable boots that would make our journey more difficult, but the reality was that basic skis are fine for the North Pole. There is no special technique required to move slowly over the ice pulling a sledge; but when you are scared, everything matters. Our fears and insecurities about the expedition ahead morphed into the belief that having the "right" pair of skis would help us.

I remember Nataša asking me advice regarding the length of the skis.

Should we aim for shorter or longer? I had no idea. I checked what my tent-mates, Lamees, Steph, and Olga were allocated. We were buzzing around over the frozen ground of the icy warehouse, looking at what every other team had for reassurance and comparison. We forgot about looking professional. Then suddenly there was a crash and everyone in the warehouse stopped what they were doing to look at us. Asma had slipped on ice in her new boots. Fortunately she hadn't hurt herself, but it was our cue to calm down and make our way out of the warehouse.

During these final weeks of hectic preparation, I felt bad that I was adding yet another burden on the team. I was responsible for committing us all to undertaking an ambitious scientific research project during the expedition, and it was already using up large chunks of our time and focus. The involved scientific protocol required the team to spend hours at a time in Longyearbyen Hospital for preexpedition data gathering. In charge of the research project was Dr. Audrey Bergouignan, a physiologist specializing in the study of metabolism and its regulation by environmental factors. She held a joint appointment at the University of Colorado, Denver, and the Centre national de la recherche scientifique (National Center for Scientific Research) in France.

Audrey is also my best friend and the person who encouraged me to apply for the expedition. I had been sitting next to her in a laboratory in Strasbourg, France, when I read the posting on social media recruiting women to ski to the North Pole. I immediately showed it to Audrey, thinking that she would be a perfect candidate, but she said, "This is not for me. This is for you. You should apply." If not for Audrey's encouragement, I would probably not have gathered the courage to start my application.

As I had read more about the expedition Felicity was planning, I started to daydream about it and chat to Audrey about what I could bring to the expedition if I was selected. As a scientist I wanted to do something that would be of value, but as a marine mammal specialist I couldn't see how my expertise could fit into the planned adventure. During the expedition, there would be humans and the ice, nothing else.

Audrey, however, quickly saw that the extreme Arctic cold paired with days of grueling physical activity was a rare opportunity to study how the female body adapts in the most demanding environmental conditions. I was shocked to learn how little information exists about extreme physiology specific to women. Since 1957, only a few studies have investigated physiological adaptations during polar expeditions, and with the exception of one female explorer, all of them were performed in men. Furthermore, most of the studies were conducted more than twenty years ago with a very small number of participants. No study had ever investigated the physiological adaptations of a large group of females undertaking a polar expedition.

This expedition was an opportunity to change that. We could add new knowledge on how women adapt to extreme environments. This drew perfectly on Audrey's expertise. She was then leading a team called Physiological Adaptations to Gravity & Health, which aimed to understand the physiological adaptations to gravity-dependent activities and their applications to human health. In other words, she studied the biological adaptations of humans to the space environment and specifically worked to assess the energy needs of astronauts while in the International Space Station. For a decade, her team had played a key role in the management of human space flight, and data from an all-female expedition into the extreme environment of the Arctic could directly inform her work. I made a deal with Audrey: if I was lucky enough to be selected for Felicity's expedition to the North Pole, Audrey would design a study for us.

I should have known that Audrey would not, of course, design a mediocre study but craft a state-of-the-art scientific investigation and assemble an international all-female team of researchers for *the purpose. She and her team arrived in Longyearbyen with nearly $100,000 worth of materials and equipment and the support of local scientific and hospital staff in Longyearbyen, who provided the facilities for the groundwork that needed to be done. The aim of the ambitious protocol Audrey had developed was to determine, as precisely and thoroughly as possible, the impact of polar conditions on the energy needs, biological rhythms, and physiological stress of the team. It involved measuring total energy expenditure, metabolic rates, and body composition of team members as well as tracking patterns of physical activity, sleep, and body temperature. Finally, it would monitor levels of the stress hormone cortisol in our saliva, as well as substances such as insulin, glucose, and fatty acids in our blood in order to reveal the physiological stress response of each individual.*

For Audrey this data represented a unique opportunity to better understand the physiological flexibility of the human body when facing extreme environmental conditions and cold temperatures—to work out how the body uses energy when under stress and how it adapts in the circumstances of such an environment as a ski expedition over the Arctic Ocean sea ice and the physical activity it represented. The knowledge would help in planning future exploratory missions to extreme environments, such as the polar regions or to space, as well as endurance sports like ultramarathons. She called the study POWER, or Physiological adaptatiOns in WomEn during a noRth pole expedition.

Vital to the success of POWER was the commitment and cooperation of the team to provide the data and undergo various monitoring. When it was proposed to the team, the response was enthusiastically positive and unhesitating. The group was curious to learn more about their bodies and keen to contribute to a study with clear purpose and legacy. Even so, as I surveyed the strained and exhausted faces of my teammates spending precious hours in Longyearbyen Hospital, I reflected guiltily that it was a lot to ask of them at such a time. Already stressed, scared, and overwhelmed by the pressures of our repeatedly delayed expedition, they sat listening intently to Audrey's explanation of the protocols they had committed to: blood test, oxygen test, body composition measurement, hormone test, measurement of resting metabolic rate, and saliva samples. Then she ran through the suite of wearable monitors that would be attached to us for the duration of the expedition as well as the samples to be taken routinely throughout. Finally, she described the postexpedition measurements required during further days at the hospital when we returned to Longyearbyen.

It felt like a lot. I began to wonder whether it had been a good idea to get the team involved in something that was such an added burden. My guilt deepened when, during our first day of testing at the hospital, Audrey's team struggled to take blood from some of my teammates, particularly Ida, who ended up being punctured half a dozen times until finally they were able to get a sample from a vein in her neck.

During another session we were given the most expensive drink of our lives—and it was water. Each of us was asked to drink a small bottle of what is called "doubly labeled water," which contains isotopes that can be traced as they pass through the body. Each bottle had to be specifically prepared for our individual body composition and was unique to each person. This is why each tiny bottle of tasteless drink cost nearly two thousand dollars! Once we drank the water, we had to be continuously monitored for the day so that the water could be tracked through our bodies. This process gave Audrey a measure of our energy expenditure as a baseline when not undergoing the expedition and would be measured again through the same process when we returned.

We were also asked to lie on a bed for an hour while wearing a mask that was hooked up to some monitoring equipment. Not a problem, you would think, especially when we were all in such need of a moment to

A few of the small monitors placed on the bodies of the team to collect data for the POWER study during the expedition

relax. But there was a catch. While lying on the bed we had to be as inactive as possible, no reading or singing to ourselves. We were even asked to keep thoughts at a minimum, yet we were not allowed to let ourselves sleep. It was a harder task than it sounds.

Finally, each of us was allocated all the monitors we would wear before, during, and after the expedition. Audrey had put a lot of effort into making the monitors as comfortable and unobtrusive as possible, but it still felt strange as we emerged from the laboratory covered in sensors. A heart rate data logger was fastened around our chests along with a temperature sensor the size of a watch battery that was taped in place above our ribs. On one wrist we had a sweatband with a sensor sewn on the inside, and on the other wrist we wore a sleep monitor. Fixed round our hips was an accelerometer and data logger, while high on the backs of our arms a fine needle was inserted into our blood stream via a patch that looked a little like the security tag on clothes in expensive shops. Altogether we felt a bit like something resembling cyborgs. It took some getting used to.

However, the thought that we were contributing so directly to new knowledge created a frisson of excitement that we all shared. This feeling was deepened by the perfect synchronicity with a second scientific study the expedition had committed to completing. Where POWER explored the body's adaptation to the extreme environment and conditions of the expedition, this second work looked at the adaptation of the mind to the same. On previous expeditions Felicity had worked with Dr. Nathan Smith, a lecturer in sports psychology at to the University of Northampton in the UK. Like Audrey, Nathan was keen to capitalize on an expedition of women with varied ethnicities in order to expand the scarce data on female subjects.

His work looked at the psychological responses, developments, and challenges individuals experience as a result of undertaking expeditions in extreme environments. The specific focus of the expedition study was to understand how the experience impacted the perspective and values of team members as well as different thoughts, feelings, and behaviors. Our contribution was to complete multisection questionnaires as a daily diary that asked for details about personal factors within the experience and different psychological processes related to how each member of the team thinks, feels, and behaves.

The connection between the two studies was the hormone cortisol. Cortisol is intricately connected to both mental and physical stress. Both investigators were interested to know the degree of correlation between cortisol levels and our individual stress levels, whether the cause was mental or physical, and the overlap between the two. And so it was vital that our cortisol levels be monitored as the expedition progressed.

Cortisol is most usually monitored in saliva samples. All the subject has to do is spit into a sample tube or chew on some absorbent padding. Simple enough—unless the temperature happens to be -40°. At the temperatures we would experience on the Arctic Ocean, saliva would freeze almost the moment it left our lips.

Audrey had put a great deal of thought into how best to reduce the complexity of what she was asking the team to do. But I could feel stress levels rise as she distributed dozens of small sample bags filled with individually labeled tubes and swabs to the team. Even I felt daunted, not least because I knew how vital it was for us to get these samples right. As the scientist on the team, I had naturally taken on responsibility for overseeing the data collection while the expedition was in progress. It began to sink in what a task it would be to coordinate such a large group of women.

MISBA: *We flew north, farther north than I had ever been before. Soon even Iceland, that bitterly cold training ground, was far to the south of us. We crossed the Arctic Circle and just kept going. Exotic places that were once merely names on a map passed beneath the wing of the aircraft: the North Cape, the Greenland Sea, Svalbard, Spitsbergen. I landed in this white wilderness to be greeted joyfully by Felicity and the team, who eagerly started sorting through the more than two hundred pounds of equipment I had brought out with me.*

Longyearbyen was almost too much to take in, a frontier town that is home to fascinating people…and polar bears. It is one thing to read about these magnificent animals but somewhat disconcerting to know that they are quite so close. All over Longyearbyen were signs warning of bears nearby, and there were enormous stuffed polar bears in the town's shops and restaurants. Whenever we went to buy food, I would stare for ages at a particularly ferocious stuffed bear in the grocery store, transfixed by the creature's enormous teeth. I had read all I could about them, learning about migration habits and how they could reach a height of ten feet when they rose on their hind legs. But the more I read, the more my fear grew.

We couldn't help but feel a little intimidated by Longyearbyen, and our surroundings began to fray our confidence. Mariam asked me to practice lighting the stove with her. After our last training expedition in Iceland, I had asked Felicity if I could take home one of the expedition stoves we had been using. At home I had practiced lighting it over and over in my garden until it became almost second nature. Finally I believed I'd become proficient at it. But now, as I went outside into the freezing temperatures of Longyearbyen to practice with Mariam, I found that I just couldn't get the thing to light.

All the old doubts came flooding back. Mariam couldn't get hers to light, either, but after a while we eventually succeeded in getting a good flame. It'll work, it'll work, I reassured myself, and then Mariam and I decided to pack the stove away quickly, not wanting anyone from our respective tent groups to see us having difficulty. Other equipment wasn't quite the same in the cold, either. The straps on the skis we were issued were different from the ones we had used before. Deciding that I needed to practice with them, I went out into the -20°C (-4°F) weather and attempted to strap them on. With all my gear on and especially my thick polar mitts it was very difficult. I could feel myself getting frustrated, and I repeatedly asked myself: How would I manage it when it was an additional twenty degrees colder at the North Pole?

MARIAM: *I felt so fortunate to share a tent with Nataša. I thought she was such a badass—and she is—but I also discovered she was thoughtful, easygoing, and hardworking. As a journalist, she always*

Mariam (left) and Nataša

had witty and often hilarious commentary ready to share. She got things done efficiently and made my stomach hurt from laughing all the while—the perfect balance you'd hope for in a teammate, especially when embarking on a challenging journey.

What you share on an expedition is different from anything you'd dream of sharing with a near-stranger in regular life. Something about the expedition experience allows you to open up more readily, to build trust. I quickly grew close to my teammates, particularly Nataša. We shared many firsts together, and in such a short span of time. We shared countless hiccups and challenges as well as many moments of pure and giddy excitement, such as when we finally got to see all the polar *explorers we've been researching online, casually strolling around in Longyearbyen. We also talked about more sentimental elements in our lives: love, family, and our pets back home that we missed.*

On the last evening in Longyearbyen before we left for Barneo, I sat with Nataša in the shared apartment where we'd been staying for two weeks. Accommodation in Longyearbyen was limited, so we'd ended up quite a way from the rest of the team. We got up together, had breakfast together, walked in and out of town to meet Felicity and the team, shared meals, and spent our evenings together. Despite the repetition, we were always up for taking the long and scenic route home to explore something new. We were in the same rhythm, appreciating all the little things that came along with this big adventure.

We spent that last evening sipping jasmine green tea and making adjustments to our gear. I had decided to do something about my ski trousers, which had become a little too big on me. I tried to sew some extra Velcro into the straps to make them fit better. I thought of my grandmother, who would have been proud of my sewing skills. I'd lived with my grandmother for the past fifteen years, and every time I traveled anywhere, she would ask me to recite an Islamic Arabic saying that translates to "May God return you safely to your destination." It was the first thing I wrote in black marker across the top of my sledge bag as I readied it for the plane that evening. I added "Be Here Now" and "Live Out of Love." They were messages that I knew would carry me on the journey ahead, and I hoped they might be seen by whoever needed to read them when times got tough.

One of two helicopters operated from Barneo waiting to transport us to the starting point of our expedition, eighty kilometers (fifty miles) from the North Pole

SEVEN

Barneo

The geographical North Pole, the point around which our planet spins, sits slightly off-center in the Arctic Ocean, much closer to Greenland than to Alaska. Its remoteness and extreme inaccessibility are demonstrated by the fact that the first undisputed claim to have reached the North Pole was as recent as 1969, when members of the British Trans-Arctic Expedition, led by Sir Wally Herbert, became the first known people to reach the North Pole across the surface of the Arctic Ocean. They had set out from Alaska with sleds and dogs and spent the winter camped out on the ice before reaching the pole and then continuing on to Svalbard—in all, a journey of some 6000 kilometers (3800 miles).

It is poignant that just three months after Sir Wally and his team stood at the North Pole, Neil Armstrong made his "giant leap for mankind" onto the surface of the moon. The fact that humans set foot on another planetary body, almost before reaching the summit of our own, speaks volumes about the complexity and difficulty of travel on the Arctic Ocean.

Today, it's no longer possible to repeat Sir Wally's journey. The margin of sea ice that extends the last few hundred miles to the coasts of Alaska and Svalbard is no longer stable and reliable enough for surface travel. The last surface journey from land to the North Pole was made in 2014, when a team skied from northern Greenland. Many believe this will never be repeated. It is not just a matter of changes in the ice but also that the vital logistics needed to undertake such journeys, in particular the air support needed to collect and return teams from the ice, is now considered too hazardous to be a reasonable risk.

There remains just one logistical operation that enables travel to high-latitude Arctic Ocean sea ice and the North Pole for ski expeditions. It is a strip of sea ice, which serves as a runway, smoothed out by a dedicated work team each Arctic spring relatively close to the pole, with a tented camp close by. Known as Barneo, the camp and runway can only be established in mid- to late-March, once the sun has returned, and must be dismantled and abandoned by the end of April, when the movement of the sea ice it sits on becomes too dangerous. This brief three-week window each year is now the only time in which surface expeditions to the North Pole are possible.

Barneo is a commercial operation, and there are already fears that financially, bureaucratically, and logistically it might soon become untenable. Without it, there will be no way to access high-latitude Arctic Ocean sea ice by surface transport such as skiing or with dogs. In a period of less than fifty years we have witnessed the first people to travel over the surface of the Arctic Ocean to the North Pole—and what might well prove to be the last.

While the opportunity for polar explorers to plant flags at the top of the world may not concern many, the story of the North Pole serves as a compelling demonstration of just how fundamentally and how rapidly the Arctic is transforming. We still hear climate change discussed in terms of a hypothetical future, yet the story of the North Pole illustrates that environmental change in the Arctic is not something that will happen at a safe distance in our speculative future, or even in the present—it is already written in our history.

After weeks of delay, my phone rang in the early hours of the morning with the news that our flight was ready to go. I rose in the half-darkness of a northern night and quietly collected my things. At the airport, as we stood waiting to board the flight from Longyearbyen to Barneo and on to the Arctic Ocean, it occurred to me that while the women around me were hardening their determination to be the first from their country to ski to the North Pole, they might also be among the very last. As one veteran polar explorer put it, "We're not chasing firsts anymore. We're chasing last chances."

STEPH: *Clutching my phone and breathing deeply, I tried to keep it together as I made last calls to my parents and loved ones. Once the final call was made, the realization of how deep my attachment was to the people on the other end of the phone set off a stream of silent tears. The cold stung my face and my fingers were going numb. I robotically began searching through my pockets for my gloves and soon registered the familiar stinging sensation of my hands warming up again.*

The hangar at Longyearbyen airport that we were using as a departure lounge, waiting to board our flight, was as cold inside as it was outside. It was haphazardly cluttered with stacks of skis and poles taped together using various team identification labels and piles of brightly colored sledges waiting for deployment. I tried to hide my tears by hanging back from the group behind a pile of storage boxes. Felicity spotted me. She enveloped me in a bear hug and I sobbed on her shoulder. I knew that as soon as I stepped on the plane I would snap into expedition mode and commit to the experience, but for now there was a knot in my throat that made it hard to breathe.

The fat-bellied Russian Antonov on the apron outside the hangar was waiting to take us to the ice of the Arctic Ocean. It was the early hours of the morning, and the moon shimmered behind the stark, jagged mountains of Svalbard, illuminating the snow. Our team was fairly chatty as we boarded, considering the time, but Mariam was awfully quiet. Her eyes looked slightly glazed and she had a stricken look on her face. We sat together in the first row of seats and I suggested she get some sleep.

Few of us had slept much over the last few days. Nataša had curled up on the row next to us, folding her long legs against the walls of the plane. She fell asleep, covered by her black down jacket. Anisa and Misba had also crashed out in the row behind us, but Ida and Asma were still chatting, as were Susan, Lamees, and Olga. Felicity was sitting in the last row and had a concentrated, serious look. Settling into my seat, I noticed that Mariam's gear had exploded across the floor in a disordered halo.

After a few hours I felt the plane begin to descend. I couldn't see out the tiny windows set back into the fuselage, but I began putting on my layers, leaving the down jacket until last, and checked the contents of my zipped pockets, mentally noting that the extra gloves were on my right. Mariam was getting ready very slowly. I hoped it was just drowsiness, but she looked overwhelmed, as if unable to switch into gear. Within moments we would be stepping out onto the Arctic Ocean for the first time and experiencing its cold. I thought back to a talk I'd heard by an ex–British Special Forces soldier while we were training for the Antarctic expedition. He had described how the shock of the extreme cold of the Arctic could prompt the mind to shut down, leaving a person unable to function. Arctic shock, he'd called it. His advice had been to mentally visualize the moment of arrival on the ice beforehand, to picture everything in minute detail and to imagine a perfect response to that moment. The point of the exercise was that when the moment arrived in reality, in addition to being physically prepared with all the right clothing and equipment, we would be mentally prepared as well.

The door finally opened and the roar of the plane's engines was deafening. We'd been warned that the plane never shut down its engines while out on the ice, in case the cold shut them down for good and the plane became stranded. A gust of Arctic wind swept into the passenger area and lingered, dropping the temperature instantly. I awkwardly clomped down the rough metal stairs in my bulky padded boots. There was no time to take in the surroundings. Instead we each had to find our sledge and skis and transport them to two waiting helicopters on the far side of the small camp. It all happened very rapidly, and in what felt like an instant I found myself sitting in the helicopter, feeling the rotation of its blades as a thudding vibration. I made a conscious effort to ignore the petrified faces of my teammates staring into space, likely thinking about the blistering cold they had just felt and wondering how we were going to cope with that throughout the long days ahead.

LAMEES: *As the day of departure got closer, I could sense the excitement and anxiety rising within the team. I tried to keep the growing panic around me at arm's length, telling myself that I was happy to live in denial if it meant I could better make the most of my stay.* Plenty of time to panic while I'm at the pole, *I thought.*

On our last night, a teammate came to see me, freaking out. "Tomorrow we leave for the pole," she said, "but I'm starting to have cold feet about it. The thing I'm worried about the most is the thickness of ice and whether we'll have enough ice to walk on."

I tried to talk to her calmly without getting affected myself. I'd had similar worries but had heard someone in Longyearbyen saying that the ice was very good this year, nearly six feet thick. I sat with her until the early hours, trying to console her as she detailed her biggest concerns. It was hard not to give in to the angst myself. Everyone was dealing with the stress and fear in their own way, no one wanting to have a negative impact on the rest of the team, but it wasn't easy.

"Remember," I told her. "This will be one of the most amazing

adventures of our lives, and we've been waiting such a long time for this day to arrive. Now it is time to enjoy it."

I continued to force myself to appear positive even as we drove to the airport for our flight to the ice. At the airport we stood in a cold hangar watching the flight crew load our packed sledges into the back of a large aircraft. This is it, I thought. No going back now. I could see in the faces of my teammates that they were struggling to know what to feel.

From left to right: Asma, Mariam, and Lamees waiting to board the plane at Longyearbyen airport

I sensed fear, nervousness, excitement, anxiety, and strength all at the same time.

I took a moment to step away from the group and find a quiet place to record a farewell video for my family in Kuwait. As I talked into the camera, I was surprised that my main response to the moment was happiness. It was time to embark on the adventure we had been preparing for. I felt relieved, almost, as if something that had been squeezing my throat finally let go and I could start to relax and enjoy the real adventure. I knew it wasn't going to be easy, but when was easy anything but ordinary?

On the plane I concentrated on trying to absorb every moment. Staring out of the window as we took off, I remembered what Felicity had told us about expecting to feel a sense of shock when we arrived on the ice of the Arctic Ocean and experienced the extreme cold of high latitudes. I tried to imagine how this extreme cold might feel and what the shock Felicity had spoken of might be like. She had prepared us to be ready to protect ourselves in those first moments when we stepped off the plane at Camp Barneo.

Suddenly it felt as if ice had entered my veins and penetrated my heart as I realized I had made a terrible mistake. When packing my sledge I had been careful to place all my warm gear—my down jacket, my thick gloves, my face coverings—on top of my equipment so they would be the first things to hand when I unzipped the sledge. I wanted to be sure that everything I needed to protect myself from that first terrible exposure to the cold would be easily and immediately accessible. But I had not considered that my sledge would be securely loaded in the back of the aircraft, beyond my reach. I could see now that I would have to get off the plane and wait in the subfreezing air some time before our sledges were unloaded. All I had was what I was wearing, two very thin layers without anything to put over my head or face to protect my skin.

Susan sat next to me, but I didn't dare share my awful secret until everyone else around us had either fallen asleep or moved away. She looked alarmed when I confided my mistake. I could see it in her eyes but her response was all reassurance.

"Don't worry, Lamees. Once we get off the plane I will cover you and the rest of the girls will stand around you to keep you warm until you get your sledge and can wear your gear."

I tried to feel relieved but kept thinking of that first awful moment stepping off the plane into the deepest cold I had ever experienced. What if it was windy? I could be severely injured in no time. As the plane landed and we all stood to leave, Felicity stopped me. "Lamees— can you put on your down jacket now, please?"

When I told her it was in my sledge, there was a moment's silence. She fixed me with a serious look. "Okay. Concentrate and keep moving to stay warm until you get your sledge," she told me, clearly worried.

The aircraft door opened and revealed a flat, white glare. I was so focused on staying warm that I didn't take any of it in. I kept telling myself, It's going to be okay, Lamees. And when I didn't freeze on immediate contact with the air, I reassured myself that it was not that bad. I just needed to keep moving. I stayed close to the group, especially Susan, and tried not to panic, focusing my thoughts only on keeping warm. Then Nataša called me over. My sledge was one of the first to be offloaded and was already on the runway waiting to be collected. Without saying a word I rushed over to my sledge, easily identifiable by the bright yellow ropes I had deliberately attached to make it stand out, and tried to stay calm as I rapidly pulled my gear out of the sledge bag and put on my down jacket.

There wasn't much time to be relieved. The rest of the team had already moved off the runway to where we could fill our fuel bottles.

Susan (left) and Lamees on the plane flying from Longyearbyen to Barneo before Lamees had her awful moment of realization

The fuel was needed to power the stoves during our expedition. I was amazed at the efficiency of everyone around me, not just the team but other expeditions that had arrived on the same flight, as well as the crew that ran the station. The activity only amplified my excitement. Soon I was pulling my sledge and skis toward the helicopter waiting for us at the edge of the camp. Our gear was loaded and we jumped onboard.

As the helicopter started its engines and lifted us from the ground, I was overcome with feeling. Out of the window I saw nothing but snow. No vegetation, no wildlife, not even birds. Snow and only snow. Inside the helicopter we all sat looking at each other, quiet, cold, and lost in our own thoughts. My head was heavy; I was very tired. I still hadn't completely thawed out from my earlier exposure and my body ached all over. I was exhausted. Glancing at my watch I realized we had all missed out on an entire night's sleep, and the hard work hadn't even started.

As soon as the helicopter landed we jumped out into the snow, turning to help each other drag our heavy sledges from the side of the helicopter and move them well to one side. Felicity called to us all to sit on our equipment in the snow, keep a tight hold of all our belongings, and face our backs to the helicopter as it took off. There was a huge wind that got ever more intense as the noise of the helicopter reached a crescendo. Then silence. The quiet fell on us heavily.

"Look," Misba said, pointing her finger around the horizon. "Look around you, Lamees. There is nothing. All you can see is white, snow, sky, white, snow, sky. There is nothing."

I took in the view. It didn't look unusual to me. It's just like a white desert, I thought. A desert without plants and huge dunes but a vast white desert nonetheless.

NATAŠA: *As we approached Barneo, the pilot announced it was -38°C (-36.4°F) on the ground. Of course, we expected the temperature to be* *that low, but it was the first time I'd heard it reported out loud as a matter of fact, and it felt surreal. Felicity had encouraged us to not be afraid of the first moments in the cold. "It might be a bit stressful. You might be overwhelmed and feel you are running out of air, but stay calm. It will pass."*

The big moment came. I stood at the top of the stairs leading from the plane down to the ice and looked around. I took a deep breath. And again. Where is this Arctic shock they were talking about? I wondered. It didn't feel so bad. I smiled as I approached the ground, thinking that if this was it, then there would be no problems at all. I could do it!

Ten minutes later my eyelashes were covered in ice and my eyelids had frozen together. I had my first moment of panic. For a split second I could not open my ice-soldered eyelids as I tried to thaw them with my gloves. This was the moment when the seriousness of the situation and the need to be 100 percent focused at all times became crystal clear to me. With all the adrenaline rushing through my body, I was sweating, which made me even more stressed since I knew sweat could freeze at these temperatures and dangerously sap body heat. At the same time I was wondering if I should go to the toilet or not.

There wasn't much time between landing and transferring to the helicopter waiting to fly us to where we would start the ski. I remembered Felicity saying something about how it was better to go as soon as possible if you have to, otherwise my body would consume too much energy—or something like that. So I ran to the toilet cubicles behind the base. When I returned the team was already loading equipment onto the helicopter. I looked around with my newly unfrozen eyes—everything felt so new. Other expeditions had got off the plane alongside us and were busy loading their own helicopter across from ours. The other teams seemed very experienced, and I wondered how we looked to them and what they thought of us—ten women with no previous Arctic experience setting out for the North Pole.

OLGA: As I boarded the Antonov, heading to the Arctic Ocean, I couldn't quite believe it wasn't a dream. We were on our way. I had been to Camp Barneo and to the North Pole once before, when I worked for an adventure travel company in Russia. The company ran VIP trips to the Arctic, including a helicopter trip to the pole, where we would stay for less than an hour. That trip was amazing, but this time I would be skiing to the top of the world instead of flying in.

The Antonov crew was Russian, so I went up to the cockpit to talk to the pilots. It was going to be my last chance to speak in my native tongue for a while. They seemed really pleased to see me and were happy to tell a fellow native speaker about the functions of the various flight instruments. They also offered me tea and candy and asked questions about the expedition. They were intrigued that we were an all-woman expedition. I ended up spending the entire flight with them.

It was fascinating to watch the different parts of the horizon bend as we flew north, all of them seeming to converge at one spot. It really did look as if we were flying ever closer to the top of the world, as if I could see the exact spot of the North Pole ahead. Finally, the pilots pointed to some dark shapes, and I could just make out a camp of large tents and a runway strip in the boundless ice desert. When we began to descend they asked me to stand behind them, and they gave me a headset so I could listen to the landing instructions.

Since Barneo is located on the unanchored skin of ice that constantly drifts across the surface of the Arctic Ocean, the landing coordinates for the runway are always changing, and the planes must be landed manually. I stood quietly as the pilots talked to each other in low, serious voices. They were both buckled safely into their seats, but I remained standing, unbuckled, with nothing to hold on to. Then suddenly, with a boom and a violent jolt, we landed on the ice. The plane jumped around as if out of control but the pilots continued to give commands to each

Having landed on sea ice smoothed by bulldozers into a runway, the Russian Antonov is emptied, all the sledges waiting on the ice to be claimed.

other in reassuringly even voices. For a few seconds I imagined that I would be the first to leave the plane, exiting through the front windshield. But with another, softer, jolt we came to a halt and the pilots were grinning at me. All was well. "That was the most unforgettable landing of my life," I said aloud.

The whole Barneo operation is run by Viktor Boyarsky, a polar explorer whose name is famous in Russia. He is a veteran of expeditions to both poles and looks every inch the explorer—a big bear of a man with wild hair and full beard. In the nineties, he came up with the idea of building this runway on the sea ice that could be used as an access point to the North Pole. It was a complicated effort and remains a complicated operation.

Each year a new runway must be built from scratch. The runway and camp can only ever be temporary because the ice beneath it moves and melts during the summer. So every spring two helicopters make their way north from Siberia. At some point, they land on the ice of the Arctic Ocean, where one helicopter refuels the other before returning, while the other continues toward the North Pole. This solitary helicopter and its crew search the ice from the air, looking for an ice floe somewhere close to the pole that is big enough and strong enough to take the weight of a cargo plane and allow the building of a runway.

When they have found a good location, a plane is sent from St. Petersburg to fly over the chosen spot on the ice and drop parachutes of fuel and supplies. It even drops a bulldozer by parachute, as well as several people who follow the cargo down to the surface of the frozen sea. A few years ago, the bulldozer landed on weak ice and fell through. Ever since, two bulldozers are dropped with separate parachutes to ensure that at least one will land safely. It is less costly to lose a bulldozer than it is to send a second cargo flight out from St. Petersburg to the North Pole.

The crew of the helicopter and those who arrive by parachute work around the clock to clear a runway on the surface of the chosen ice

The pilots of the helicopter at Barneo. The helicopters provided vital search-and-rescue cover should something go wrong, as well as transport between Barneo and the North Pole.

*floe, using the bulldozer to flatten small pressure ridges and areas of
ice rubble. They must work fast because the window of opportunity for
ski expeditions on the ice so far north is very small. Before mid-March
there is no daylight, and temperatures are so cold that aircraft and
other mechanical equipment cannot work. By the beginning of May the
ice has already degraded and weakened to the point that it is no longer
safe for planes to land or for teams of people to be traveling over the
surface of the sea ice. So Barneo usually opens in early April, when the
polar day of constant light has begun but the temperatures are still
low and the ice remains strong. Three weeks later, the camp closes. All
expeditions must be completed and all people and equipment removed
from the camp before it is too dangerous. In order to get the maximum
amount of time, the crew must work quickly to get the runway
operational as soon as possible each April.*

*All this effort for a few weeks of possibility! Going to the North
Pole is a dream not so easy to achieve. Imagine that first plane landing
on the new runway of ice—what an anxious moment. The first flight
brings supplies so that the camp can be built, as well as more people to
help transform a deserted ice floe into a small village. There are large
heated accommodation tents where expedition members and tour guests
can sleep overnight, as well as a large mess tent where people can sit
down to meals cooked on-site by a camp chef. There is a generator for
power, a staff doctor with basic medical facilities, and even a sauna for
the pilots and crew.*

*Despite being built on an ice floe very close to the pole, Barneo
will often have drifted sixty miles or more by the time the short season
is over. The ground crew at the camp must constantly monitor the
condition of the ice as it moves gradually southward in a clockwise
direction around the pole.*

*Of course, there were no saunas or chef-cooked meals for us when
we landed. We went straight to the helicopter for the second leg of our*

Arctic flight. And all this happened at night. It was 5:00 a.m. by the time our helicopter landed on the ice floe where we were to start our march on skis. It was -35°C (-30°F), but in the first minutes I didn't feel it. There was no time to stay still and listen to my feelings. We had to unload our skis and sledges and check that everything was in place and in order before the helicopter left us. My joy became euphoric. The moment we had spent so long waiting and preparing for was happening and I was living my dream. The North Pole was waiting for us.

Struggling to find their rhythm as a group on the first day, the team drew out into a long unsynchronized line.

EIGHT

The Arctic Ocean

Rather than a fixed geographical feature, sea ice is a terrain that is ephemeral in every way possible, relentlessly changing in form, stability, position, extent, even molecular state from moment to moment. It is a landscape of constant change, a thin layer of frozen sea trapped between the movement of the currents and tides of the ocean below and the wind and weather driven by the atmospheric circulation above. It is not a solid boundary but a pliable membrane flexing at the whim of the conditions that surround it.

From the helicopter I could see the spidery patterns of pressure ridges—places where the action of wind and sea swell had forced ice together, pushing large plates and boulders of ice rubble up onto the surface so that they formed vast barriers. There are no markers of scale on the Arctic, no buildings, trees, or geography against which to judge the size of a thing, but I knew pressure ridges could be as high as a room and miles wide. From the air they looked like erratic scratches, forging onward as far as the horizon. I traced theoretical routes through and around the worst entanglements of debris, but I imagined how the landscape would appear when faced on foot without an aerial overview: an incomprehensible maze of impenetrable obstacles seemingly without end.

More daunting still were the great dark gashes where ocean and atmosphere had conspired to force the ice apart to form leads—narrow channels of black open water revealed between broken sheets of ice. In places the leads had begun to refreeze, the different thicknesses of new ice creating overlapping leaves of translucent gray in deepening shades, while in others the ragged edges of ice had been pushed far apart so that leads became lakes. These broad spans of water were often cluttered with white islands of pack ice broken free from the rest, clustered together like giant jigsaw pieces. From the air it appears possible to cross this open water by moving from one cracked remnant of ice to another. But on the ground, without an elevated overview and with no maps of these ever-changing features, such a decision would be a blind leap of faith, with no way of knowing if one direction or another would lead to a watery dead end.

Everything was moving. Not just the ice splitting open and refreezing, or ice pressing together to agitate the rise and fall of ridges, but entire pans of pack ice tens of miles across jostling against each other, all set within an ocean-wide skin of ice that was itself swirling with the rotation of the planet, churning and grinding in a configuration so complex that humankind has yet to map or predict it in anything but the broadest of terms.

The Arctic is the smallest and shallowest of the world's oceans, but what makes it truly unique is its frozen surface that (as of yet) never completely disappears. In winter the ice cover expands, spilling through the Bering Strait and extending southward through the Fram Strait between Greenland and Svalbard, with a solitary tendril extending along the eastern coast of Greenland almost as far south as Iceland in the north Atlantic. In summer the ice cover shrinks back, receding from the coasts of Alaska and Eurasia to form a condensed mass somewhere north of Greenland. This annual ebb and flow is a natural rhythm of passing seasons in the northern hemisphere, the heartbeat of our planet as it circles around the sun.

Huge slabs of ice protrude from the floe, revealing the thickness of the sea ice.

For decades, satellites have been used to monitor the seasonal expansion and contraction of Artic sea ice. Watching ice fill and then empty from the Arctic Ocean is like watching the rise and fall of lungs—as if we are observing the planet breathe. As the images run through the years to the present day, the swirling mass of Arctic ice dissipates like a smoke ring, almost to nothing. When displayed as a graph, this data forms a jagged line like a child's drawing of a range of perfectly pointed mountain peaks, with each peak and trough representing the annual growth and contraction of sea ice across the Arctic. Some years the peak is a little higher or lower; other years the trough might be a little deeper or shallower. This is the natural variance from year to year in the amount of sea ice cover. You don't need to be a scientist, however, to spot that the whole mountain range is on a clear tilt. It starts out at 1979, in the top left of the chart, and rapidly heads toward the bottom right-hand corner of the present day. If you study the chart closely you will also see that the gradient of the downward slope is getting steeper, meaning that the trend it reveals, of decreasing amounts of ice, is accelerating.

Not only is there less sea ice cover on the Arctic Ocean than ever before, but what is there is newer, thinner, and less stable.

Sea ice is generally categorized as one of two types: first-year ice and multiyear ice.

First-year ice has formed the previous winter and is in its first summer. Multiyear ice has survived at least one Arctic summer. No one knows exactly how old the oldest ice in the Arctic Ocean might be, but it is estimated that the majority of sea ice is discharged through the Fram Strait into the Atlantic less than ten years after forming. Working on a Russian nuclear icebreaker crashing back and forth across the Arctic Ocean between the North Pole and Murmansk on the Siberian coast, I was taught how to tell the difference between first and multi-year ice. If the melt pools that dotted the surface of the ice floes like stains of spilled ink were the blue-gray color of the Atlantic, then the ice was relatively thin and likely to be first-year ice. If the pools were the turquoise blue of the Caribbean Sea, then the ice beneath them was relatively thick and almost certainly multiyear ice.

There are other clues, too. If the ice is flat and smooth, it is new. Older ice becomes disfigured by the eroded remains of pressure ridges, scored with the pockmarks left behind by old melt pools, or covered in a spiky display of shards and rubble where it has collided with other ice forms and amalgamated into one. Multiyear ice has been around long enough to have a history indelibly displayed on its skin. On the Russian icebreaker, I watched as the weight of the vessel's immense hull crushed the sea ice and turned it over in the water as it was pushed aside. While the new ice, three feet thick at most, was easily broken, the multiyear ice often produced blocks the size of one-bedroom apartments. It is the rapid disappearance of this stronger, thicker multiyear ice that is arguably more concerning than the decline in the overall surface extent of the ice. The older ice breaks apart less easily and acts as a cement that holds the entire Arctic pack together. Without it, the Arctic ice cover will dissipate more quickly and more completely and will take longer to re-form, if it does at all. The ultimate consequence is a summertime ice-free Arctic Ocean, which would have far-reaching, fundamental consequences on every global environmental system, from the depths of the deepest ocean to the heights of the upper atmosphere.

The year of our expedition, the US National Oceanic and Atmospheric Administration reported that the proportion of older ice in the Arctic Ocean had declined by as much as 95 percent since records began. This is deeply concerning for environmental scientists trying to predict the impact on the planetary environment. It is also pretty disturbing for any polar explorers about to embark on a journey over that ice.

As the helicopter set us down on a wide, smooth pan and the team stepped out onto the pack, I felt as if a stopwatch had been set in motion. The ice beneath our feet was constantly moving. The individual floe on which we stood was being propelled by ocean and atmosphere, but so was the entire ocean of ice that surrounded it. If we took too long to reach the North Pole, we ran the risk of being carried by the drift into a position where we would have to battle against the movement of the ice to make any forward progress—like skiing the wrong way on a conveyor belt. I had no way of knowing how quickly or in what direction the ice beneath us was moving, and until the team started skiing, I had little idea how swiftly we would be able to move as a group through the terrain or how long it might take us to reach our goal. I had no intention of turning our expedition into a route march, but to remain stationary now felt like a bad choice.

However, I was also aware that the team had missed an entire night's sleep and was running on little more than nervous energy and adrenaline. We had the option to pitch our tents and get some rest, but it seemed clear to me that we needed to move—even if just a little—to prove to the team that we were capable of facing the challenges that lay ahead and to dispel the pall of intimidation created by the cold and the view around us.

I gathered the team together in a huddle and explained the options. "I need you to be honest with yourselves and with me about how you feel. If anyone has any doubt about pushing on now, then there is no question, we stay." Anisa was first to respond. "I feel fine. I say we go." As others nodded agreement I found it hard to tell whether they were expressing their opinion or simply going with the majority. I got the impression that many were bemused by my asking the question in the first place—the intention had always been to make the most of every second we had on the ice. Besides, the cold was beginning to bite and the quickest way to get warm was to ski.

As we had drilled so many times before, we formed two lines, each of us on long cross-country skis with ski poles roughly the height of our chests, and harnessed to our own sledge that trailed a few paces behind. Having fluttered about making sure everyone had snacks and water accessible, hands and faces protected against the cold, sledges tightly lashed, flare guns and rifle for bear protection in place, I took my position at the front of the line, strapped my boots into their bindings, and with a glance over my shoulder at the team lined up behind me, took the first steps north.

More than two years of relentless effort had led us to this precise moment. I reflected on the periods of intense stress and worry when the expedition had appeared an impossibility and stalled in its tracks, on times when we had pushed onward with our plans despite little reason to hope for fruition—and yet here we were. Two years of determinedly preparing the team in every way possible in order to earn this opportunity to be setting off together to ski across the Arctic Ocean to the North Pole….

Yet everything began to fall apart almost immediately.

We had trained to move together in a tight-knit group and maintain a slow and steady pace that left no one struggling to keep up but was swift enough for us all to stay warm. We'd established a routine of skiing for around ninety minutes before taking a short break, each of us taking turns to lead the group at the front of the line. The larger the group, the more important it was to have clear routines and systems so that everyone knew not only what they should be doing at any given time, but what everyone else around them would be doing, too.

During our first training expedition in Iceland we had struggled to make progress across the glacier, the line stopping every few minutes while someone adjusted clothing to prevent themselves from overheating or getting too cold, to find something they needed that had been neatly packed away in a sledge, or to adjust their boots to avoid any uncomfortable friction points turning into blisters. These were all perfectly justified reasons to stop skiing, but at each pause, others in the team would seize the chance to put on some lip balm, munch on snacks, step aside to have a pee, or adjust their own clothing layers. The pauses would quickly cascade into lengthy stops, and it was tough to get the group moving again. Inevitably some would get perilously cold waiting for others to be ready to continue.

Over time we became practiced at doing most things on the move, from adjusting clothing to applying sun cream, or by simply putting up with whatever the irritation was until the next scheduled break. As we each got to know better how our bodies reacted to the environment and our activity levels, it became possible to preempt a lot of issues. Rather than setting off wearing multiple layers and feeling comfortably warm, we learned to make sure we felt a little chilly when we started, knowing that we would soon be producing plenty of body heat once we got going. Even our bodily functions eventually began to fall into the rhythm of our routine so that we only needed to pee every ninety minutes.

So it was frustrating on that first day when, after just a few strides

Susan taking the lead as the team skis through a small line of ice rubble on the Arctic Ocean

on the Arctic Ocean, the line stopped. The plastic of our ski bindings had hardened in the cold and became difficult to tighten properly. The problem was made worse by the fact that most of the ski bindings were designed for large masculine feet. Asma's boots kept slipping out of the bindings, making it impossible for her to slide the ski forward. As soon as we came up with a fix to solve the problem, we were stopped again by Steph having the exact same issue, then Lamees, and then Mariam, then Asma again. Soon I was tackling issues up and down the line, aware that we were not getting enough time between stops to allow ourselves to warm up properly.

I drew comfort from the fact that regardless of what else was happening, the team were doing what they had been trained to do in order to look after themselves and each other—checking on their allocated "buddy," putting on their puffed down jackets for warmth each time we stopped, constantly eating from pocket snack bags, and moving on the spot to keep their circulation pumping. Yet there was no disguising the heightened anxiety. It ran through us all like static electricity—unseen, unspoken, but tangible.

In the Arctic, the only way to get warm is to take action to make yourself warm; the only way to find shelter is to build it; the only way to keep moving is to will yourself forward. Such depth of responsibility for our own well-being requires shifting into an alternate mental gear. Steph had experienced all this before, yet even she was gripped by a sudden terror that caused her to forget everything she knew about facing the challenges of the cold, just as Lamees, who was experiencing the polar regions for the first time, was momentarily immobilized mentally and physically, perhaps by the enormity of what we were confronting.

Ida and Olga had the most experience in similar environments, so I positioned one at the back and one in the middle of the line of skiers, while I tried to set as slow a pace as I dared at the front. I was trying to close the distances that had opened up between skiers without anyone getting either too cold or too overstretched. We had become badly unsynchronized, with those at the back catching up just as the ones at the front, who had been waiting, got too cold and were forced to move on. The line of skiers expanded and contracted like a pulse moving along a spring. The sheer size of our group vividly demonstrated its capacity to be a problem—and not only were we a team of eleven, but we were being shadowed by the five members of the film crew as well.

As I glanced back, I noticed that Holly and her crew were right

Susan taking a break on her sledge

behind us. My heart sank as I imagined their frustration at our inability to stay ahead of them as planned. I was upset that on the first day, our performance as a team was not representative of our hard-earned capability and everything I was so proud of. I considered calling a halt to set up the tents, but our confidence as a team was more diminished than ever. I could sense it all along the line. I needed to keep us going, to build up that confidence. I was the one who had told these ten people that we could do this, and now was the moment I had to prove it to them.

After our next stop, I asked Susan to take a turn navigating from the front so that I could spend more time moving up and down the line of skiers trying to evaluate how everyone was doing. I skied next to Mariam for a while. With ice crystals coating her eyelashes like glitter, she was in breathless awe of the parade of exquisitely sculpted ice that we skied on by. "I didn't expect it to be so colorful," she said. Mariam has a knack of elevating perspective, of unveiling meaning in details that might otherwise be missed, without it feeling pretentious. For the first time that day I actually spent time taking in our surroundings and enjoying the moment. I felt transported away from all the pressure and restored for a little while to a place of confidence and calm that was more familiar. Mariam's soulful personality was the reason I had known we needed her on the team. She inspired everyone around her to see more, to feel deeper, to appreciate everything.

Next, I checked in with Ida and immediately sensed her frustration. She was having trouble with her skis and was annoyed that it was limiting her ability to help others as she was used to doing as a guide. I had worked with Ida on expedition ships in the Arctic before and knew her technical capability. I had also come to know her as someone who was brilliantly strong-willed and competitive, particularly with herself. Her usual good cheer was strained, and I suspected that she would rather be alone with her frustration. Working back up the line I stopped with

Misba, her face fixed in an expression of determination that it had maintained all day. "I'm tired, but I'm okay," she told me after a long moment of consideration. Head down, gaze focused on the back of the sledge in front, she had rigidly maintained her position in the line, just a few back from the front, ever since we'd set off. I suspected that retaining her position in the line was Misba's way of assessing how she was performing. Or perhaps she was worried that if she fell back, she wouldn't be able to catch up again. Unbreakable resolve and nervous insecurity radiated from her in equal measure. I'd come to recognize this uncommon mix as her defining characteristic. She was a person of great ambition and strength who nevertheless openly battled constantly with doubt and fear. I admired her not because of her achievements but because I could see plainly the courage and effort those achievements had taken to accomplish. Witnessing Misba constantly pushing herself in spite of fear or self-doubt was a continual source of inspiration to dig as deeply as she was.

Finally we managed an hour and a half of more or less continuous skiing, and I called a halt for a group break. It was the first time we had come anything close to what we had rehearsed during our training. The team was still far more spread out than was ideal, but it was a vast improvement on our first hours of the day. *One more leg*, I thought to myself. *Then we can stop.* But as we set off again, Ida abandoned her troublesome ski and resorted to using just one, pedaling with her free foot as if she was on a skateboard. I hated seeing her struggle. Mariam too, when her binding failed once again, abandoned her skis altogether and took to walking. I appreciated their determination to continue, but it was obvious that to limp on in this fashion was counterproductive.

When we emerged onto a broad pan of ice wide enough to allow some distance between us and any significant areas of rubble where there might be cracks or movement in the ice, I crossed my ski poles over my head to signal a stop. The team gathered round and I shared the good news with them: we had covered almost exactly eight miles from our drop-off point. This wasn't far off the tentative target we'd set ourselves for our first day, and it was a surprise that despite all the problems and delays we'd experienced, we'd managed to achieve it regardless. I'd expected our mileage to be a lot less. Tiredness was forgotten for a moment as we celebrated and I battled not to get emotional at the sight of the confidence restored in the faces around me. I hoped it showed in my own expression too. Finally, we believed what we had been telling ourselves to believe for so long. We believed we could ski to the North Pole.

A short while later, as I gratefully crawled into the tent I shared with Mariam and Nataša, Mariam asked, "Felicity, will you take a look at my hands. I'm sure it's nothing but I just want to be sure."

She pulled off her mitts and both our faces fell in shock. Above thin, angry red lines that circled her finger tips, the flesh was gray.

It was frostbite.

MARIAM: *The moment we got inside the tent, my body let go. I began to shiver violently and couldn't make myself stop. Felicity quickly got the stove going to heat the tent, and gradually I began to remove my multiple layers of clothing as the air warmed up. I took off my gloves and looked again at my fingers. The tips were as white as snow. I knew the moment I saw them that it wasn't right.*

"It's definitely frostbite," Felicity said. "We won't know how bad until tomorrow. If your fingers turn reddish tomorrow, that's a good sign. If they turn blue, it's not so good."

Either way, I needed to be medically evacuated. It was the last thing I wanted to happen. I was still shivering, and everything felt hazy. So much was happening and I knew I needed to focus, but all I wanted to do was curl up and sleep. Felicity told me to get into my sleeping bag and stay near the stove for maximum warmth, but as I began to doze, she reminded me of the danger of hypothermia. If my core body temperature fell too low, I could slip into a coma. Sleeping could lead to death. I was instantly very awake!

The next morning, I peeked at my fingertips inside the sleeping bag. They'd turned blue. In the darkness of my sleeping bag, I began to cry. I didn't want to show anybody my blue digits because I was scared of what it meant. When I heard Nataša stirring, I looked out from my sleeping bag and whispered, "They're blue."

I was devastated that I had to leave, but I also wanted to stay strong for my team. I didn't want my injury to affect anyone negatively. I tried to hold back my tears as I hugged my teammates good-bye on the way to the waiting helicopter. The helicopter had arrived to take me back to Barneo, and Nataša came with me to the door, the rotors beating the wind over our heads. After we hugged, I looked her full in the face. "You've got this," I told her, and I knew that she did.

I sat alone on the helicopter and forced myself to look out of the window as we rose from the ground and flew away. It was so hard. The tears that I'd fought now flowed freely and would not stop. Flashes of memories of my time with the team wrestled for space in my head.

When I arrived at Barneo, Victor, who was in charge of operations at the runway, greeted me. I had met him before, just days ago, as I had hurriedly made my way across Barneo with the team, dragging our sledges from where we had landed by plane on the runway to where the helicopters waited for us nearby. Now, as he helped me off the helicopter, he could see my puffy eyes filled with tears, and he enveloped me in a big bear hug. He took off his gloves and gave them to me. "These are the best gloves around and they are yours now," he said. I felt cared for.

Then he asked me, "Do you want to go back home, or wait here and meet your team at the North Pole?" My mood immediately lifted and my eyes lit up. It had never occurred to me that I would have such an *option and there was not a moment's hesitation in deciding to stay. Victor smiled. "Good choice," he said.*

I was taken straight to see the doctor. The medical facility turned out to be a corner of a large tent and consisted of a table littered with an assortment of medications and two benches. Above them was hung a crooked sign with the word doctor written on it. You're at a camp floating on ice in the middle of the Arctic Ocean, *I reminded myself.* Things work a little differently here. *I was told the Russian doctor at the camp had a lot of experience treating cold-weather injuries. Besides, as I reminded myself, he was the only working doctor on the Arctic Ocean. His opinion mattered.*

I sat on the bench and waited. I felt very vulnerable. I held my damaged hands outstretched in front of me and played through my memories of the previous day in my head. Where had it all gone so wrong? The day had been a long one and I had known the temperature was really cold. My body isn't used to such temperatures and I'm known to have cold extremities, even in the Saudi heat, which is habitually closer to 40°C above than 40°C below! But I had been careful not to take off my gloves at any point. I did remember that I had started to feel particularly cold about halfway through the day. I had felt my fingers getting cold and stiff, and when I mentioned it to the others they had encouraged me to remember our training—to keep moving and get the blood circulating to stay warm. I followed the advice and slowly stopped feeling the cold in my hands. Great, it's working! *I thought. With the discomfort gone I could focus instead on enjoying the surreal surroundings.*

Finally the doctor, a tall man with a gentle smile, walked in. He grabbed my right hand firmly and took his time analyzing each finger, while saying nothing but sighing over and over again. I squinted my eyes and clenched my other hand, squirming in my seat as I tried to tolerate the discomfort as gracefully as possible while he inspected my

Mariam (right) at Barneo camp on the Arctic Ocean with one of the staff members who looked after her during her recovery. Despite the language barrier, she felt welcomed into the tiny community on ice.

injuries. Suddenly he turned toward me and mumbled what seemed like gibberish. It took me a moment to realize that he was trying hard to translate words from Russian to English. My eyes widened as I waited for his verdict about my hands to become clear from the jumble of words. Finally, he abruptly announced, "No chop!"

I gulped.

Okay. That option hadn't been on my mind at all.

Even so, it was great news. I got to keep my fingers.

NATAŠA: *The snow creaked like crushed polystyrene under the rubber soles of our chunky insulated boots as we moved around the tent setting poles into place. It was really too cold to stand still for very long, so we kept moving constantly, quickly exchanging a few sentences as we passed by each other on our busy circuits around the emerging tent. Mariam kept repeating how cold she felt.*

The first day had been undeniably tough. The helicopter had dropped us off in the early hours, and we'd marched for a full day on very little sleep. We had trouble as a group, needing time to adjust and get into the rhythm of moving together, but what I'd feared most, the cold, hadn't felt so bad. I had been cold all the time but not dangerously so—or so I thought. Of course I was tired, and I rolled my eyes at the thought of everything that awaited us once we had set up the tent, from melting the snow to make water to cooking, then the laborious task of drying our gloves, face coverings, and neck gaiters which had become iced during the day—the list of tasks felt endless.

I was tired but I was also happy. We were finally on our way to the North Pole and the day had been a good start. At first, I didn't worry much about Mariam. I was sure she would get warm once we got in the tent and that everything would be all right. Yet I also knew that Mariam rarely complained, so I had a nagging sense that something wasn't right. As soon as the tent took shape I encouraged her to get inside and warm herself up, telling her it would take only a couple of minutes to get warm and that things would get better quickly.

There was still snow to be put around our tent to anchor it to the ground and keep out any wind, so I focused on helping Felicity with that while Mariam went inside to set up the "kitchen." We were all busy doing something despite being tired and cold and wanting to warm ourselves up as soon as possible. When it was finally my turn to crawl into the welcoming shelter of the tent I noticed immediately that Mariam was shivering and that she still had her gloves on. She said, "I'm still not feeling okay." Nothing seemed to help. Felicity was last in and straight away asked to see Mariam's hands. As she examined Mariam's digits, I could see from the look on Felicity's face that it was serious. The tips of Mariam's fingers were pale and turning bluish. Frostbite.

Frostbite is what happens when extremities get frozen. Flesh contains a lot of water, and it will freeze exactly as any cut of meat will in a home freezer. It is possible to freeze any part of the body, but extremities have less blood circulating and are harder to keep warm. Our fingers, toes, and faces were our main concern, but if any patch of skin was left exposed to the superlow temperatures, it could freeze and become an injury. We were taught that the best policy was to avoid getting frostbite by keeping our skin covered up at all times and making sure to monitor our extremities.

Part of our routine was to check ourselves and each other at every break in the skiing. We had a buddy system that paired everyone with another person who would scan their faces for any sign of a problem and make sure they were looking after themselves. The first sign of frostbite, we were told, is an unnatural-looking whiteness that becomes a raised patch on the face or an area with clear demarcation to the discoloring, such as the tip of a digit. It's hard to notice this happening on your own face without someone checking for you. And it's hard to notice it on toes when they are inside socks and boots. Our best defense was to ensure that we could feel every toe on our feet and had sensation in all our fingertips as well as our facial features. When you're cold, it's actually harder than you might think to establish whether or not you can actually feel something in a specific spot of skin.

We'd been shown the gruesome consequences of frostbite. As the frozen parts thaw, the skin turns purple and blue, swelling to form ugly, fluid-filled blisters. As the injury heals the skin dies, and in extreme cases extremities have to be amputated to stop infection spreading or poisoning the blood. It terrified me.

We had talked tirelessly of frostbite and cold injury during our training. The lectures had left us in no doubt of the reality of the risk, yet I have to admit that I never really considered the possibility that it would happen to us. As I continued to scrutinize Felicity's face, waiting for her to say something and trying hard to read her expression, I felt terrible for Mariam. I couldn't begin to imagine how she was feeling. I felt distressed for Felicity, too, suspecting that the weight of being responsible for the whole team must have been particularly heavy in that moment.

I hadn't spoken much to Mariam during that first day. We'd exchanged a few words during some of the breaks in the skiing, and Mariam appeared to be having a good day. She had been keeping an easy pace with the rest of the group and gave no signs that anything might be wrong. She didn't say or do anything that had struck me as concerning. With a hollow feeling in the pit of my stomach, the thought occurred to me that, although we had maintained our buddy checks on each other throughout the day, every single person on the team had been under pressure from the start, struggling with the equipment, fighting to get used to the environment and our situation in it, trying to establish the expedition rhythm. We had all been mostly concerned with ourselves that first day.

Felicity spent a long time examining Mariam's hands. "You won't be able to continue the expedition. We need to evacuate you," she said finally. I felt numb. My heart was beating so fast, I didn't know what to do. Instinctively, I looked down at my hands. The light in our tent was filtered by the green of the tent fabric, tainting everything with an odd hue that made it difficult to see color clearly. I examined all my fingers individually and minutely. I couldn't see any blisters and nothing approaching the blue that was so clear on Mariam's hands, but after a while I became convinced that on three fingertips of my left hand there was an unnatural paleness.

What was that!

I was afraid to show my hands to Felicity. Would she judge that I too had frostbite and had to go home? Was I ready for that? Eventually I mustered the courage to tell her and waited for her diagnosis. "Frostnip," she said. "Not as bad as frostbite. You can manage it but you need to take really good care of your fingers from now on to stop it getting any worse."

I was one step away from frostbite! My thoughts raced wildly. I didn't understand how this could have happened. Sure, I felt cold during the day, but not too cold. I thought that I'd had everything under control the whole time. There and then the seriousness of the expedition revealed itself, and I was so afraid. I didn't want to go home. It was not an option. I had invested too much in the project, I had worked too hard to go home now.

This can't happen, *I told myself.* Do whatever it takes. *The thought of being unable to complete the expedition plunged me into a bad mood, and I was so preoccupied with myself in those moments that I almost forgot about Mariam. She was still shivering and we couldn't seem to get her warm no matter what we did. Nothing helped. We prevented her from sleeping, concerned about the possibility of hypothermia, but tried to make her comfortable.*

Mariam didn't panic, but I saw that she was sad. She covered her face with her hands at times and cried. We didn't talk much, but the silence said everything. Instead of celebrating how we had managed to get through the first day, the hardest day, there was instead a feeling of sadness, disappointment, and frustration in our tent. The worst part was that there was nothing to be done to change any of it. Mariam was such a great teammate and a wonderful person. She didn't deserve this experience. I felt bad for her but at the same time I was so afraid for myself.

Our teammates in their tents pitched close by didn't have a clue about the calamity unfolding. I could hear the sounds of them minding their own business, preparing dinner, drying socks, getting warm, celebrating the achievement of our first day on the ice. The contrast with the reality in our tent made it even more depressing. I didn't sleep much that night, preoccupied with the thought of my frostnip and waking up every hour or so to gently massage my fingers with some soothing infant skin cream that I had brought with me and willing that my hands would look better in the morning.

When we woke Mariam's hands did not look any better. The color was deeper and the swelling more pronounced. Felicity had given her plenty of painkillers, but it was clear that Mariam was already in severe discomfort. It was obvious now, in a way that it hadn't been the evening before, that there was no chance Mariam could continue with the expedition. How would she pull a sled and hold ski poles in her aching hands? The simplest tasks would be as hard as hell, and her injury would only get worse as time went on. I realized what a good thing it was to have Felicity with us with all her experience in a situation like this. We couldn't afford to take any chances. Although Mariam desperately wanted to stay, we both knew Felicity had made the right call to evacuate her.

Everything went wrong that morning. I had never spilled anything in the tent and hadn't had a single accident of any kind during any of our training expeditions, but that morning I messed up with my coffee, spilling it on our sleeping mats. Then, when I went out to the loo, the bib of my salopettes fell right where it would have been better not to. So instead of me calming Mariam in her moment of greatest distress, she was the one calming me down instead.

I had endless questions for Felicity about what would happen next, but at the same time I didn't want to complicate the situation even more. I could see that the focus now had to be on getting Mariam to safety. A few hours later a helicopter arrived to collect her. When I heard the buzzing above us, it was hard for me to hold off tears. Mariam and I hugged, and the rest of the team joined us. I wished her all the best. I knew her energy would be sorely missed on the team and particularly in our tent. She handed me the flag of her country, and I promised to do my best to deliver it to our destination at the top of the world so that she would be with us all the time, even if not physically. We were both crying. It was not at all how we had envisioned the start of our journey.

The team crossing one of many obstacles out on the ice

NINE

#

Emerging from the tent into the cold and the light, I paused. I needed to let everyone know about the helicopter that would be arriving shortly to transport Mariam to Barneo. Instead, I wandered away from the camp, needing a moment to compose myself. The shock and emotion I'd been keeping out of my voice and expressions around Mariam now poured out privately into the snow and the ice. Anxiety for Mariam, devastation on her behalf at having to leave after so much hard work to get here, and, most of all, guilt that I had failed her. It all came crashing together.

I was annoyed with myself for the tears but then remembered something Audrey, the scientist investigating our cortisol levels, had told me. Apparently crying is the most efficient mechanism the body has for correcting an imbalance of cortisol. Put simply, when under stress—mental or physical or both—cortisol levels rise, and the quickest solution is having a good cry. I was comforted that my tears served a real and practical purpose and were not a sign of weakness after all. Standing in the ice, I didn't need a saliva swab to know that I was stressed. It felt good to visualize leaving my unwanted excess cortisol where my tears had fallen, and I returned to camp knowing I was thoroughly rebalanced.

The helicopter departed in a fury of noise and loose snow with Mariam on board along with Holly, who had decided to accompany Mariam back to Barneo. I returned with Nataša to our tent, which now felt horribly cavernous for just the two of us. As we both moved around the tent packing away equipment, Nataša slowed until she eventually stopped and covered her face with her hands. I knew what a close and supportive relationship Nataša and Mariam had formed, but I was taken aback by how hard Nataša was taking their separation. I had never seen her vulnerability before.

The reaction was about more than just the shock of Mariam's injury and the loss of the emotional support of their friendship. Nataša had been extremely physically fit all her life and had never found any physical challenge particularly difficult. Yet the previous day had stretched all her reserves, both physically and mentally. She wasn't used to having to dig so deep, and it must have been scary for someone as strong and capable as Nataša to suddenly find herself so challenged.

I was worried that Mariam's injuries and departure to Barneo might also have a destabilizing effect on the team and undo all the great work we had done to build up our confidence during our first day. But it actually seemed to have the exact opposite influence. As we set off that second morning, we were completely unrecognizable as a team from the day before. Instead of a long shuffling line, we skied steadily as a close-knit group in two parallel lines, each set of ski tips falling just short of the sledge in front, as we had trained.

Encountering the first few lines of rubble on the ice, the team seemed to float through them fluidly, as one, each teammate finding her own route of least resistance through the boulders and shards before we all coalesced again on the far side. It was beautiful. The film team, who I had worried had been annoyed by our slow pace during our first day, told me that morning that they had in fact struggled to keep up and had been frustrated by our speed. "You told us this wasn't going to be a route march," they complained. I was struck by the irony of my misapprehension. The camera operators, Kathryn and Ingeborg, wanted to be able

A partially frozen lead on the Arctic Ocean

to mingle within the group far more than they had the first day so they could capture the footage they needed, and that meant traveling more closely together than Holly and I had originally planned. Not for the first time, I reflected that managing the expedition was a constant balancing act that never seemed any easier to get right.

The line stopped. Susan was leading and I skied to the front to find her staring into a dark blue lead at her ski tips. Even if there wasn't a minute that went by without thinking about its presence so close under our feet, to actually see the ocean was alarming. As I watched, the cleanly sliced crack in the floe widened smoothly. What had been the size of a small stream was quickly becoming as wide as our skis were long. "Don't get too close," I warned the team instinctively as they came to have a look at our first lead.

Scouting for a better place to cross, Susan found a good route over a small pressure ridge that led to a neighboring floe. Gathering the team, I described the plan briefly and we started to cross, working together to get each person and her gear over quickly, one behind the other, before the ice beneath us had a chance to move or separate. I made sure I was the last to cross, but only by the tiniest millisecond, eagerly following the last team member in front of me. I didn't want to be the one left behind any more than anyone else.

The next lead we encountered was frozen. The water had already solidified into a layer of dark gray ice, blooming with tiny, delicate flowers of frost but uncovered by snow. Again, stopping the team in a huddle, I cautiously surveyed the crossing, first striking the ice with a ski pole before tentatively testing it with the weight of one ski-laden foot. Nothing moved. We crossed two at a time, spaced apart but in quick succession. Everyone was silent, listening for any slight crack or noise that might herald a shift in the ice. We heard nothing except the glide of our skis.

I looked at the ice passing beneath my boots. I had spent weeks skiing over the surface of frozen lakes in Siberia and Scandinavia on past expeditions, but the quality of the ice on the Arctic Ocean was distinct from anything I had come to know before. No light filtered through it, the depth of its color suggesting the depth of the sea beneath. I felt a little pang of regret as I watched the metal edges of my skis flatten the gardens of frost flowers, leaving nothing but a dusty trail of ice crystals behind me.

As we encountered and crossed more and more frozen leads, we grew less cautious. Over time, the precrossing consultations became briefer and the assessment of safety more rapid, but we were never far from a reminder of the danger of complacency. As we passed over one thickly frozen but relatively wide lead, the noise we all feared rang out from beneath our feet—a shattering crack. The whole team froze for a moment, our senses suddenly so taut it was painful. Half of the team shot forward to the safety of the snow-covered ice on the far side of the lead, while the rest flashed back the way they had come. We all felt our hearts in our mouths. When the ice showed no movement or further noise, a ripple of nervous laughter rose from both sides of the lead as we swiftly regrouped to move on.

Later, we came across a pan of ice littered with eroded ice blocks and boulders. Ahead a mist appeared, hanging low like a ground fog. I knew it meant there was open water somewhere close by. Despite air temperatures hovering below -20°C (-29°F), the temperature of the ocean beneath the ice is considerably warmer. Sea surface temperatures cannot get colder than a few degrees Celsius below zero because of the salt content of seawater. When the ice breaks open to expose the subzero water of the ocean to the even colder air that lies above, the resulting condensation is known as sea smoke—the exact reverse of a steaming bath.

Against an overcast sky, the sea smoke cast an eerie melancholy and left me with the impression that we were weaving our way through the monuments of a frozen graveyard. A shiver went down my spine that had nothing to do with the cold. When I saw what caused the smoke, I didn't lose the sense of foreboding. Bordered by thick, contorted slabs of ice, a dark area of open water came into view. The surface was already slushy with refreezing, but the darkness of the water was horrifying. I muttered my relief that we didn't have to cross this particularly grim laceration of the ice.

The pressure ridges were no less nerve-wracking. Like fault lines between tectonic plates, these blockades of irregularly shaped boulders and slabs, inherently unstable, were heaped over the boundaries between ice floes. Any movement of the sea ice under a pressure ridge could send the teetering mound of ice rubble tumbling. Imagining what might happen if we were in the middle of negotiating a pressure ridge when it moved compelled us to make our ridge crossings as quick and efficient as possible.

However, the ice proved to be as mesmerizing as it was unnerving, and it was difficult not to linger. The ice could be as clear and smooth as a lump of undulating glass, angular and striated, slashed with varying shades of blue or as opaque and white as porcelain. The intensity of color was endlessly astonishing, particularly in the gaps between boulders in the rubble. The same gaps that threatened to trap legs and arms with a single slip also captivated us with glimpses into concentrated tones of blue that transformed into greens and even the richest purple. The ice reflected the sunlight, which was itself a spectacle at that time of year at such a high latitude. The sun never approached the horizon but gave the impression of being too sluggish to reach a zenith. Instead, it circled us in a strange altitude of compromise somewhere between the light of dusk and dawn, and it stained the sky in a near-permanent wash of pinkish yellow.

Some ice boulders on the sea ice—not just white, but every shade of blue possible

Some of the pressure ridges we could cross with our skis on and remain connected to our sledges—though this often required brute force and determination to strain forward in our harnesses and force the fat sledges over rough ground or through narrow gaps. More usually, the rubble was so tightly packed that it was impossible to negotiate with our long skis. We'd take them off and scramble over the ridges on foot—rarely an elegant process. We sometimes found ourselves awkwardly astride great slabs or sprawled over mounds, bruising knees, elbows, and shins as we shuffled from one position to another. Frequently one person could not get herself and her sledge across a big pressure ridge alone. Instead, each of us would shove hard at the sledge in front, then turn to heave at the sledge behind. Sometimes the team would form a chain across a ridge and pass one sledge at a time from group to group in a relay. The size of our team, which at times had felt like a disadvantage, proved it could be a blessing too. More hands made lighter work, and we became increasingly efficient at the task.

IDA: *When you think of skiing the last degree of latitude to the North Pole, it is tempting to consider only the straight-line distance of about seventy miles.* Not very far, *you might think. But skiing on the Arctic Ocean is not remotely like skiing in any other part of the world. On a flat surface you might ski fifteen to twenty miles a day while hauling a sledge behind you—but the frozen Arctic Ocean is a terrain of open leads and pushed-up ridges, and the ice is always moving. When nature has forced you to ski all day to progress just two miles, you know you are on a strange corner of our planet. We certainly did. There were times we felt we were never going to get anywhere.*

When we reached our first major pressure ridge, I climbed to the top to see if I could find a way to get through, but all I could see was a maze of ice boulders. There were no flat areas anywhere. Felicity and I went off alone to see if we could find a safe route through the maze, but wherever we looked it was the same impossible jumble of ice debris. Returning to the team, Felicity told them we would have to work together and help each other to get over the ice, carrying the sledges one at a time, taking off our skis if needed. The ridge was about thirty feet high. It was amazing to think that it was created purely by the force of plates of ice being pushed into each other, building up into immense mounds. On the Arctic Ocean the ice was alive and really wild.

The team lined up within the chaos of ice boulders and began heaving the sledges up and over, passing skis and poles from one to the other. We had already fought very hard against the ice and the cold that day. Despite the physical effort and our technical polar clothing, we were not impervious to the temperature. The icy wind was like a sharp knife scraping my cheeks. The cold can make you tired, angry, or sad, and for some it is misery, though not for me. The cold gives me strength and makes me alert. It keeps me alive. Many think of the Arctic as a very quiet place, and it can be, but if you listen closely you can hear that the ice is full of noise and movement: the sound of cracking, of friction, of splitting. There is nothing like it.

The ridge took over two hours to cross. That evening we were quicker than usual getting into our sleeping bags. I spent some moments, as I did every evening, writing in my diary. Starting with the coordinates of the camp from my GPS and the date and time, I recorded what I had eaten and what my feelings and thoughts had been through the day. Often I didn't write in full sentences but just jotted down words that described the impact an experience had had on me—not what the ice looked like, for example, but how it made me feel. For many people, ice is something to slip on that causes cars to skid and crash. To me it is the source of miracles. Ice makes it possible to ski on water, to cross seas, to reach the top of the world. Ice is cold, blue, wet, fragile, brittle, hard, angry, fearful, white, tensile. It can be slicing and savaging, but it is also cooling, calming, and freeing. Ice can destroy and injure but also

Felicity on the ice after scouting ahead for the best route forward

protect and form destiny. It is the inspiration I draw from the ice that keeps me coming back to the Arctic for more.

OLGA: *The first time we came across an open lead, it looked like a river with vapor rising over it, creating an illusion of hot water. It was an incredible sight, eerie and beautiful at the same time. I felt the urge to dip my fingers into the still surface to feel its temperature. As we watched, smaller cracks appeared in what was seemingly a solid surface, branching from the open lead. The ground beneath our feet was alive and fragile. It made me feel both uncomfortable and excited. This was the Arctic I had read about.*

We found a place to cross, and although the lead looked relatively wide and the ice more fragile than I would have liked, my childhood experiences of crossing frozen bodies of water meant that it didn't strike me as particularly hard or dangerous. Even so I was cautious, testing the ice ahead by hitting it with my ski pole before each step. I

At the start of every day on the ice, the team gathered together to discuss the plan and our progress. From left: Steph, Susan, Olga, Ida, Anisa, Asma, Misba, Felicity, and Nataša.

kept my other hand on the carabiner that connected the sledge to the harness around my waist, mentally preparing to disconnect myself with lightning speed should the ice crack beneath me. I was glad we had done the ice-breaking drills in Iceland—even though at the time I had thought them crazy. I felt reassured that, should the ice crack open, not only would I remember what to do to get myself out of the water, but I also knew what my teammates would be doing to help. They would be finding a safe place to pitch a tent and doing everything necessary to help me to get dry and warm quickly, to avoid frostbite or hypothermia. With that in mind, my worry eased and my confidence grew.

Later, our first serious pressure ridge towered toward the sky and stretched across our way like a barricade. At first I thought we could ski alongside and then around it, like contouring around a hill. But it was an illusion. Like the end of a rainbow, the apparent end of the pressure ridge always hovered just ahead of us, forever out of reach. We skied and skied, every step taking us farther from our route due north, until it became clear there was no end. Instead we had no choice but to portage directly through the ice rubble.

As we negotiated the awkward scramble over heaped boulders and slabs of ice, the group would pause and I would be sent to scout the route ahead. It felt wonderful to move for a while without the weight of a sledge. I felt so light it was almost as if I bounced across the ice, like an astronaut on the moon. My delight was tempered, however, by the thought that my freedom from the sledge was only temporary. The harness was always waiting.

As leads and pressure ridges became more familiar, I became more confident and acclimated to the Arctic environment. It is in my nature to lead, and soon I felt ready to head up our skiing procession. The first time I volunteered to be at the front of the line, I skied alongside Susan. It was a pleasure to work with her. She was in control of time, direction, and pace, and all I had to do was to ski confidently alongside her and look for the best route around any stretches of ice rubble we encountered. The next time I volunteered to lead it was without Susan, and I had to be in control of everything. It was surprisingly challenging. The relentless responsibility to be in control of so much was more tiring than the physical exertion of skiing. There was so much to think about, and I really had to concentrate hard for the full ninety minutes.

Even so, I liked being in the lead. I enjoyed looking for the routes of least resistance through the rubble and picking out landmarks that would lead us north. Sometimes landmarks were easy to spot, like an iceberg we spotted on the horizon one morning. It had never occurred to me before that icebergs did not always float free in the oceans but could be locked within the sea ice like this one. It was amazing to see this

*giant, as big as a multistory building, frozen in the middle of the pack
ice, making all the other enormous slabs and shards look like miniature
colorless crumbs in comparison. For days we were able to navigate
toward its dark bulk as it lay, conveniently, directly north of us.*

*At other times there were no such obvious landmarks, just the
endless fields of rubble. Then I would have to rely on the GPS that I
kept warm by tucking it into my mitt or down the front of my jacket. If
I let it dangle on the lanyard around my neck the batteries would run
down within minutes. I relied a lot on my intuition to lead us north as
well, but since we nearly always skied in pairs, I could confer with my
companion if I wasn't sure we were heading in the right direction.*

*The challenge was not just to keep on a northerly track. We also
had to find safe passage through the pressure ridges, leads, and other
obstacles without making too many extended detours away from our
northerly bearing. When navigating for the team, I had to strategize
when it was best to bear left or right or straight ahead. Making
continual microdecisions was exhausting and stressful. Often a decision
would turn out to be the wrong one, and having led the team into a
pressure ridge, everyone struggling to clamber over slippery ice chunks,
heaving our sledges along in our wake, I would spot that tacking left or
right would have been the better choice. Or even worse, to notice that
the lead we had just risked our safety to cross ended a few yards away.
Sometimes I wondered why the team ever trusted me to find the right
way.*

*Once we spent a whole day looking for a safe passage through a
particularly extensive stretch of rubble. We worked hard for many
hours but made very little progress. At one point, Felicity and I left
the team to scout ahead and look for signs of a better route through
the barricade. I scrambled to the top of a large ice boulder to get a
better view. I stood, sheltering my eyes from the glare of the sun and
the wind, squinting at the strange landscape of the pack ice, and as I*

concentrated on trying to make sense of it, I became aware of a tingling sensation at the back of my neck. For an instant it was as if I could see this precise moment in time from the outside, as if seeing myself through the eyes of a teenage me. I was in the Arctic going north to the pole. I was scouting for a passage through the ice ridges, surrounded by great teammates who trusted me. I could have been a character from the movies of polar exploration that I had seen in my childhood. My lifelong North Pole dream had taken shape and been made real, and that reality was wonderful.

In that moment, standing on a boulder, it didn't matter whether we would ever stand at the precise point of 90 degrees north or not.

Lamees carrying a bundle of skis through a pressure ridge the team is in the process of crossing—never a straightforward operation

The journey we had experienced so far, as a group and as individuals, learning and overcoming the day-to-day trials of the polar environment, had already turned me into a polar explorer—the sort of explorer I am proud to be. That moment on a boulder was when I felt I had truly achieved my ambition.

NATAŠA: *It was perfectly sunny as the whole team turned to the task of packing up our camp after Mariam's departure. Everyone secured their various cargo in the sledges, ready to be hauled for another day. Now that it was just me and Felicity sharing our tent, we divided the equipment Mariam had been carrying between us. Other teammates kindly came to our aid as well, taking on extra weight on their own sledges to help us out. There wasn't a scrap of free space on our sleds.*

When I tried to pull my sledge with its additional weight, it didn't move at all. It was so heavy. I thought I might be able to drag it for an hour or so, but how could I do ten hours or more? The first steps felt like I was dragging an elephant along behind me. I fought back feelings of rising panic as my thoughts raced from the helicopter that had taken Mariam away to my injured fingers and back to the impossibly heavy sledge at my back. Calm down! *I ordered myself. I couldn't afford to panic right at the start.*

Part of the problem was that my sledge was not very well balanced. I hadn't managed to pack the equipment evenly, so that the sledge would not overturn. Yet no matter how I rearranged the contents (and even when Felicity tried a few different methods of packing it), the sledge continued to roll repeatedly. Imagine how inconvenient it is to turn around on your skis, breaking whatever rhythm you have managed to build in your stride, negotiating icy and uneven terrain as you backtrack a few yards to heave upright a dead weight? Then to set off and a few strides later have the same thing happen again…and again and again and again?

"*Why are you doing this to me?*" *I would yell at the sledge. It was hellish, and my teammates following me weren't happy about it either. Misba in particular, who had by chance ended up skiing behind me each day, knew of my troubles with the sledge all too well. At first she scolded me for my frustration, telling me to be kinder to the sledge, talk to it nicely, don't be too harsh….*

Yadda, yadda, I said to myself.

Sure enough, after three days of skiing behind me and repeatedly helping me right my overturned sledge, Misba told me in all seriousness that if I didn't throw my sledge out of the helicopter on our way back, she was going to do it!

As time went on I felt real hatred for my sledge. Sometimes I couldn't hold back and would pummel it with my poles, giving it full force to vent the frustration and using some strong words in Slovenian. Needless to say, it didn't help in the slightest.

No one except Felicity knew about my frostnip. I didn't want to tell anyone else for fear of affecting morale in any way. But during those first days, all I could think about was the state of my hands and whether the next helicopter would be for my evacuation. During the day I frequently changed my gloves to keep my hands warm and dry, while at night I woke regularly to massage cream into my fingers. Stopping the frostnip from turning into frostbite became all-absorbing. I didn't dare take out my camera to take photos or videos of the surroundings. It seemed a small sacrifice in comparison to the healing of my injury and my continued place on the team.

At the end of day three, Felicity and I were in our tent—just the two of us in the tent now—and although Felicity never gave me any cause to think it (her manner was admirable at all times), I couldn't help feeling a little like a student sharing a room with a teacher on a school trip. I was aware of being on my best behavior at all times, perhaps trying to prove myself. I found myself cooking and operating the burner in front of Felicity and was worried she'd pick up on my reluctance. I felt under pressure to be absolutely perfect.

This particular evening Felicity had taken control of the kitchen. It was wonderfully warm and we'd just had a very satisfying rehydrated meal of spaghetti bolognese, which was quickly emerging as a favorite. I knew that my fingers were in much better condition. The white blotches had almost entirely disappeared and no red or blue bruising-like color had appeared. I wanted Felicity, as someone who had seen something like this many times before, to confirm it for me.

She took a look. "You are fine," she said, "your hands are looking good. Well done, Nataša." Finally I could say that I had the situation

Nataša working through the regular end-of-day routine in the tent: chores, science, diaries, self-care, sleep

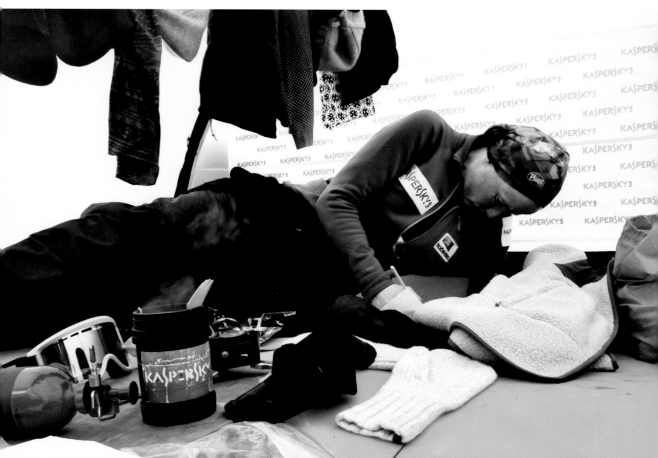

under control. I felt instantly more relaxed, and as I got myself comfortably wedged inside my sleeping bag, ready for sleep, I looked forward to enjoying the journey the next day—and reporting on it.

STEPH: *Having pain, itching, or any sensation in extremities is fine. It is when you can't feel anything that you have to worry. As we were skiing, I realized with a sickening feeling in my stomach that I couldn't feel my fingers no matter how much I wiggled them. Without stopping, I clasped both ski poles under my arm and shook first my right arm, then my left, as vigorously as possible trying to get the blood moving and into my fingertips. I stepped out of the line to attempt star jumps on my skis in the snow as furiously as possible, thinking that if my whole body warmed up then so, surely, would my fingers. My hands refused to warm and I couldn't feel any sensation at all. It was as if a switch had been flicked off and my hands had disappeared completely. Panic began to set in.*

Suddenly Lamees was next to me. She grabbed my wrists and forced my hands through the open zip of her jacket, placing them in her armpits. I stared into my reflection in her mirrored goggles and repeated manically, "I don't want to get frostbite. I don't want to get frostbite."

Felicity appeared with an emergency pair of warm down gloves from her sledge, and I became aware of the growing group of concerned teammates around me. Ripping off my mittens, which had become brittle with all the frozen moisture in them, I shoved my hands into the emergency down and propelled my arms like a windmill to warm up. I was still repeating the same words and had lost all sense of self. Felicity grabbed my shoulders, pulling my face close to hers, looking at me straight in the eyes. "Steph, you haven't got frostbite. You need to calm down." I tried to explain that I'd never experienced anything like this before, that my body was not reacting as I expected it to. But as the warmth seeped slowly back into my fingers, my energy drained away, and with it my panic.

View of the team's tents from the periphery of the camp taken on bear watch.
This was about as far as anyone wandered from the tents alone.

TEN

Keeping Watch

Each evening I would pull out a hand-drawn map my husband had given me as I left to catch the plane in Longyearbyen. It looked like an image of a dartboard, with the North Pole as the bullseye. Lines of longitude radiated from the center, and concentric circles indicated lines of latitude. It was our only map and, despite being so rudimentary, it was of huge importance to me. It enabled me to visualize our progress, which supplied a regular boost to morale.

At each of our camps on the ice, I made a small blue blob on the map to mark our position. As the days passed, the blue blobs formed a knobbled line from the top right of the dartboard toward the bull's-eye. The forward progress toward the pole was our own, but the movement clockwise around the dartboard was caused by the drift of the ice beneath our skis. Though we weren't in any particular hurry to reach the North Pole, if we took too long to reach the bullseye, we risked the ice moving us into a position where we would be carried steadily away from goal—a situation known as negative drift. The map was a reminder that we couldn't afford to hang around on the ice unnecessarily; we had to keep moving.

I dreaded checking my GPS each morning, anxious about how our camp had moved while we slept. I feared waking to find that the ice

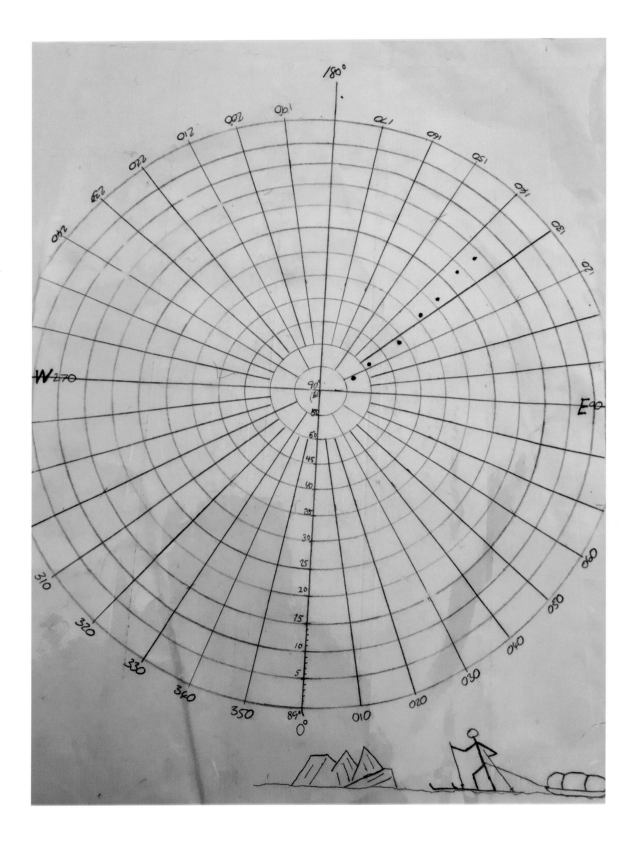

had carried us away from the pole. Having the distance to our destination grow overnight would have been incredibly demoralizing. On most days I would find that our camp and the ice floe it sat on had indeed moved a few miles while we slept, but fortunately it had moved almost exactly sideways—no closer to the pole but no farther away either. It felt like a good compromise. However, on one precious morning I turned on my GPS to discover that we had moved two and a half miles *closer* to the North Pole…without taking a single step! We'd done nothing to earn it, but it felt like a victory.

Each day brought us closer to the pole and also made us stronger and more determined as a team. We fell into a confident rhythm, and I enjoyed how my role changed within the group. I had been clear with everyone from the start of the project that I was not their guide. Instead, my mission as the leader of the expedition was to provide each team member with sufficient training and opportunity to amass the skills, knowledge, tools, and confidence to become competent polar travelers in their own right. I did not want to guide the team to the pole—my aim was that, if and when we successfully reached the top of the world, each person would know that she had done so due to her own capability, and that we had made it as a team on our own terms.

For every person to have that satisfaction and to be able to go home with that pride in what she had achieved was important to me. There were many times, however, that I questioned my approach. Initially, as the team met and tackled the training expeditions, my role had necessarily been one of instructor. I took care of everything, from teaching the team the routines and systems I had developed on previous polar expeditions, to making sure everyone was eating and drinking sufficiently, to mending broken bits of gear and finding solutions to problems,

Our only map. The hand-drawn illustration might not have been a brilliant navigational aid but was an important source of motivation.

big and small. It is exhausting to take that level of responsibility and impossible to keep it up for such a large team for long. However, as the team—individually and as a group—gained experience and got more practiced, the balance of control and responsibility shifted. Eventually, not only were team members able to look after themselves; they also took greater ownership of the expedition, taking an active role in decision making, implementing new routines and systems that improved on what was learned, and making the expedition their own.

It was a moment of pride for me when I was able to stop telling my team, "You can do this," because they were now telling themselves, *I can do this!* The balance of control and responsibility, always shifting throughout the life of a team or an expedition, is a tough one to get right, and I was constantly weighing my desire to encourage others to take more responsibility against my duty as leader to draw on my greater polar experience to inform decisions and keep everyone safe. As I saw my teammates grow in confidence on the ice, I was reassured that I must have got that difficult balance right at least some of the time. I was impressed by the leadership they each showed in varying ways—on the ice, on bear watch, and in their support of each other.

MISBA: *At school, whenever a question was asked, I would never put my hand up to answer, even if I thought I knew it. I just wasn't confident enough. Halfway through the expedition, I finally raised my hand.*

As we stood around that morning, clipping into skis and harnesses, getting ready to go, Felicity told me it was my turn to lead the group. I blanched with dread but realized that this was my chance to answer the question that had caused me so much anxiety when I had first spoken to Felicity: given the chance, would I ski at the front, the middle, or the back? Despite all the training and practice, as well as Felicity's explanations of navigation, leading the group was still my worst nightmare. Back home, I couldn't even follow the satellite navigation system in my car (much to the amusement of my family), so how on earth was I going to lead the team to the North Pole?

Yet I knew that I needed to face this fear and decided to take the plunge. Shuffling to the front of our group, which had already lined up in two short parallel rows, I took the helm and navigated for the next ninety minutes. It felt exhilarating to be in charge, even though the responsibility was huge. I didn't want to get it wrong and make the team work more than they had to. Though the GPS dangled on a lanyard around my neck, I gripped it tightly so that I could fix my gaze on the screen at all times, worried in case I veered in the wrong direction. I set a good, comfortable pace, but the GPS was hard to follow. The digital compass needle on the screen that pointed north meandered left and right. Looking back constantly to check on the team following in my tracks, after a while I noticed the zigzagging trail we had left behind us in the snow.

Eventually Felicity worked her way up the line to ski next to me. She told me what I had already been told many times before in training: pick out a prominent feature on the horizon and ski toward it. Don't rely so much on the GPS. But it wasn't easy. I would spot a distant block of ice that I imagined to be the shape of a fish or a horse, but when I got near it didn't look anything like that, and I would wonder if I had mistakenly focused on the wrong ice block. It was as if my mind was playing games. I tried using the sun for direction, as we'd also been taught, but I found that even more confusing. By the end of my ninety minutes I had a horrible feeling that I had added a significant distance to the team's ski due to my lack of skill in navigating.

Later that day Felicity told me it was again my turn to lead. I welcomed having another go, but now it felt like the stakes were higher. We'd moved onto flatter terrain with fewer obstacles, giving us a great opportunity to make up for lost time. I had a nagging feeling that the right thing to do was to step aside so someone whose strengths lay in navigation could make the most of the good conditions. None of us wanted to ski any farther than we had to, and my leading might create extra distance. But if I refused, I felt I would be letting down Felicity and the team, not to mention the many people back home who were counting on me to be an inspiration.

I skied alongside Susan at the front. She helped me pick out features on the horizon to aim for. Cracks in the ice gave me time to look at the GPS, and I discussed with Susan which was the best route around. Despite the challenges, I enjoyed going over cracks and ridges. The cracks reminded me of the lines in my hands and on the faces of people I see when I work in hospital wards. I always think the lines you see on old people's faces tell you the story of their lives. Just like the cracks in the ice—except the ice would melt in the weeks to come and by next year it would all be new.

The pressure ridges were beautiful. Their startling blue interiors looked as though someone had dyed the ice, giving it an unnatural, almost eerie appearance of a fluid moment suspended in time. Even so, crossing them was exhausting and didn't even provide the satisfaction of covering much ground to show for all the effort. We were constantly taking off our skis and forming a human chain to drag and sometimes lift the sledges over higher ridges of haphazardly piled ice boulders. The sledges would regularly get stuck, wedged between irregular shards of ice or overturned by the uneven ground, leading to more exhausting delays. I worried about my sledge, conscious that I carried the precious cooking equipment. The fuel can was constantly being banged about, and I worried about leaks.

On one occasion, as we were waiting to cross a ridge, we heard explosions beneath us, like the sound of bombs going off. My brain told

Misba hauling her sledge on the sea ice

me: It's the ice breaking up! *Shaking with fear, I charged off on my skis, anxious to get as far as possible from the noise. I don't think I have ever skied so fast—but the team, all equally unsettled by the explosions, had no trouble keeping up with me!*

Once we were moving again, the only sound was the noise of our voices and the swish of our skis. The views were the same everywhere— sun, mist, sky, snow, and ridges. At every pause in the skiing, I dipped into the bag of snacks in my outer jacket pocket. I was working so hard to pull my sledge that I didn't feel cold—in fact I felt hot and sweaty even though the balaclava I wore had frozen hard in the extreme cold and my nose was always dribbling. The handkerchief I kept in a pocket had also frozen rock solid.

By the end of the day, having retaken my place somewhere in the middle of the line of skiers, I was filled with a sense of satisfaction. My fiftieth birthday was approaching and I was skiing to the North Pole. I might not have been an expert navigator or leader of teams, but I had done really well. I felt energized at living my life the way I wanted to. I felt inspired by the team around me and knew that although I had already lost weight, and although my sledge felt ever heavier, I felt stronger than ever—and truly thankful.

IDA: *For several years before our North Pole expedition, I had lived and worked in Longyearbyen as a snowmobile guide, taking guests on trips to observe polar bears. As a hunter in Sweden, I already had a gun license, but I had also taken a course on polar bear behavior. From a distance, a bear shows up as yellow against the snow, and it is important to know how to tell the difference between a polar bear and a lump of yellow ice. I experienced many encounters with polar bears in the wild and was all too aware of the risk and danger of meeting a polar bear out on the ice.*

Firing at such precious and magnificent wildlife is an absolute last line of defense and only ever considered as a last resort. Formerly polar bears were rarely, if ever, encountered within the highest latitudes of the north. Instead, they would remain around the ice edge, the region where solid pack ice erodes into the ocean, with its concentration of seals, the main prey of polar bears. Nowadays, however, the nature of the pack ice has changed. Open water can be found at almost any latitude, meaning that seals and polar bears can venture far beyond the ice edge.

The chances of coming across wildlife at the last degree of latitude to the North Pole were slight. However, just the previous year a commercial ski expedition had been stalked by a bear. The team remained safe, though the bear was eventually killed. The team had been torn apart by recriminations, and the guide was heavily criticized. The incident was a warning for us to take the hazard seriously, however unlikely its possibility, and to be as prepared as possible.

The responsibility of keeping the team safe from bears was always on my mind. While skiing I habitually looked for tracks or signs of any wildlife, especially polar bears. I made sure my rifle was always close by, strapped to the top of my sledge, easy to access and half-loaded in readiness. As we climbed across pressure ridges, it was tempting to only look down at what our feet were doing to make sure we didn't fall or get caught between ice blocks. But I made sure I looked up. As often as I could I scouted the area, always on the lookout for the significant three black dots that are the telltale signs of a polar bear—its nose and eyes. The possibility of meeting the King of the Arctic was always on my mind but particularly while climbing over the ice rubble. Polar bears prefer to hang out near debris on the sea ice, and we would have a very slow and difficult route out of the ice maze if we needed to flee.

Bear watch was another critical part of the expedition's safety—and I loved doing it. The sun would be shining and it felt crispy outside. I always dressed warmly but could still feel the cold breeze against my

Ida in the tent working on her skis

cheeks and the sound of the wind mingling with the gentle murmur of the ice blocks moving and rubbing against each other, like a northern lullaby. I felt the weight of the rifle on my back and knew it was prepared, half-loaded. The flare gun was at my waist. When I was sleeping, I had the rifle close by, easily accessible in case a teammate on bear watch raised the alarm.

Our bear-watch rotation meant that on alternating days each of us was woken for our slot of scouting for changes in the ice around camp, any new cracks, and of course for those three black dots of a bear on the horizon. When it was my turn, I would put on my skis as quietly as possible so as not to wake any of the sleeping team and move away from the camp a little, skiing in a wide circle around it but never too far away. At 2:00 a.m. the sun was still high in the sky. When I looked around at the vast landscape that surrounded our three small tents, it was magical, more spectacular than I had ever expected. It was irregular but beautiful, bold and gloomy, natural and unspoiled, arid and windswept, surreal and unfamiliar.

Despite all my adventures across the polar regions and in Svalbard, this was a completely new world to me and more distinctive than anything I'd ever experienced: the big frozen heart of the north—frozen, yet in constant change. I let my gaze roam the ice-blanketed landscape, over the rafts of floes pushed together by the movement of the pack and built up into ridges. It was an endless snowy desert, one that we were going to conquer. We were confronting the challenges of the ice, not fearless but with respect. As well as our bodies, our souls would glide over the tops of the ice ridges, bound in our self-belief that we could each succeed and in the knowledge that our potential was far greater than the confining visions prescribed to us by the world that all too often decrees how you should live your life. To stand and look at that landscape was to experience an exquisite moment of freedom and to feel empowered as never before.

OLGA: *From the moment our tents were pitched until we rose the next morning, we had someone outside the tents on bear watch. We did ninety-minute shifts before fetching someone else to take over. At first I wasn't happy about it. I wanted to crawl into my warm sleeping bag instead of marching around the camp in the solitude of the cold night for an hour and a half. I considered the chances of us encountering a polar bear to be very small. It is very unlikely to meet a polar bear so close to the pole. They hardly ever appear in those latitudes due to the lack of food.*

The second reason for our watch was to keep an eye on ice conditions. I didn't find this a convincing argument, either—though I had to concede that the possibility of a crack appearing in the ice near our camp was at least more probable than the arrival of a polar bear. I had heard stories in which cracks in an ice floe had developed right under tents, forcing people to evacuate with all their equipment and supplies immediately to avoid falling into the ocean. The sea ice felt as solid and reliable as rock, but standing still I could watch our position move on my handheld GPS device, proving that the ice floe was moving with the drift. Still, my brain remained skeptical, somehow refusing to comprehend that we were on floating ice and not solid ground. It was easy to feel immune to the dangers, especially in such a big group.

In the beginning, the bear watch was a burden, except for the first ten minutes, which were interesting. Everyone was sleeping and I was completely alone. I walked around enjoying the views. The ice chunks that lay on the outer edges of our camp were crystal-clear blue and even in the watery light of the Arctic spring sparkled in the sun like diamonds. They were so beautiful. Having glanced around to check there was no one to see, I tasted the ice, curious to know if

A crack in the ice floe close to camp. The open water in the lead had refrozen, but it was a startling reminder how close the ocean lay beneath our tents.

it was salty. It wasn't. Disappointingly, I could detect no taste at all, just a slight stickiness as the chilled surface stuck briefly to my tongue.

After circling the camp three times, I got bored. I decided to build a wall for the bathroom. Not that we needed it, but it was something to do, and I wanted to build something in the middle of the nothingness. It was a curious instinct. I don't usually leave marks of my existence on my surroundings. If I go hiking in the woods or climb mountains, I make sure to leave nature in the same way I found it. But in the boundless Arctic open spaces I felt differently. Maybe it felt too empty? I don't know. In any case I knew that my creation would disappear without a trace after a short while. I wondered if this instinct to build was the same instinct that drove ancient people to create cave paintings in order to leave some mark of their existence on this planet. I stood back to view my completed construction. Glancing at my watch, I saw the whole thing had taken only fifteen minutes. Now I had absolutely nothing to do and I still had an hour to kill.

The hour dragged on, and it felt like my watch would never end. Yet within a few days, bear watch became my favorite pastime. It was my private time, when I didn't need to go anywhere or do anything. It was a chance for me to stay still and take in the Arctic, and I began to look forward to my watch. I could wander around and look at the beautiful ice hummocks, observing how the colors shimmered and changed from white to blue. For me, to stay still and look at the ice was a sort of meditation. Soon, I would gladly have taken on additional watch time if I hadn't needed my sleep in order to be prepared for the next day.

I am an introvert. I need alone time in order to rest and recharge. I need solitude and quiet. Eventually, I became protective of my time on watch. One night, having looked forward to wandering around in solitude, I noticed a couple of teammates outside the tents taking in the view and the ice. It was hard to resist the urge to tell them to go to sleep and not disturb my solitude. I turned and walked away in the opposite direction, seeking a more perfect isolation.

STEPH: *"Wake up, Steph, wake up." Susan's voice pierced the thick fabric of my sleeping bag and the wool of my beanie hat. Eyes still closed, I groaned, fumbled for the zip, and scrambled out of the tent as fast as possible, wearing just my thermal base layer and socks. I grabbed the spare, oversized, black down jacket that was much thicker than mine and zipped it all the way up to my nose. Locating my little portable music player, I pulled the down hood tightly over my head, keeping my beanie on for extra warmth.*

Outside, blinded by the sunlight, I blinked repeatedly until my eyes were able to focus and adjust to the overexposed icescape—a world I knew was mine alone for the next ninety minutes. I walked slowly around the camp, following the deep footsteps imprinted in the snow from the numerous polar bear guards before me. My eyes prickled in the cold and my nose ran, despite being well covered. I swung my arms casually to keep the blood flowing, but before long little icicles formed on my eyelashes. I'd perfected my pace by this point, ten slow steps then stop. I stared hard into the distance, scouring the white expanse as I tried to spot any movement or shadows, eyes strained and focused for a few seconds on each portion of the imaginary sections I divided the horizon into. A few minutes into my shift, I switched off my music to enjoy the glorious silence and bask in the beautiful white pristine environment.

I broke from my usual circuit around camp and followed a set of lonely footprints heading in a straight line toward a large outcrop of ice rubble. I reached my destination to find an unexpected message carved into the ice from an unknown polar bear guard: SMILE! it read. I burst into giggles. Deciding to explore some Tetris-like ice blocks on the far side of camp, I could clearly see some rectangular shapes stacked on top

of each other like an elaborate game of Jenga. These blocks were truly impressive, the deep-blue ice under the light dusting of snow sparkling fiercely in the sunlight, highlighting the contrast of colors. I didn't dare get closer, as I couldn't assume the wall of ice was stable.

I resumed my normal circuit around camp and felt satisfied that I'd had my moment as an explorer and been able to appreciate the

Skyscape over distant ice rubble on the Arctic Ocean

environment without any intrusion. My ninety minutes were up. I quietly thanked the horizon for not producing any polar bears on my shift and said my farewells to the sky and ice, which were both now turning a pale orange-pink hue as sunrise approached.

The team skiing past a huge iceberg frozen into the sea ice

ELEVEN

High Ice and Hard Truth

Waking to start our seventh day on the Arctic Ocean, I was cautiously optimistic that our next camp might be at the North Pole. We were less than six miles in a straight-line distance from 90 degrees north, but as we set off over granular snow across a spectacularly flat expanse of ice, I detected an ominous shadow on the horizon. I silently pleaded for it to be a trick of the light and for the smooth ice that we were gliding over to go on forever—or for at least the next six miles—but within a few hours there was no disguising the fact that we were approaching a massive blockade of ice.

The jagged silhouette of the pressure ridge extended as far as we could see in either direction, and as we reached the outer edge of the rubble and scrambled up a tower of boulders for a better perspective, it was clear that it wasn't a ridge at all but a thick band of contorted, treacherous chaos. This unstable mass stretched undiminished to the northern horizon, and there was no possibility we could get ourselves and our sledges into it, never mind across. It was a particularly cold day despite the unobscured sun casting long shadows from a cloudless sky, and I could feel the team moving instinctively on the spot to maintain their body heat and circulation as they waited expectantly for a plan of action.

I was momentarily paralyzed by the weight of impossible decisions. The North Pole lay directly ahead of us, yet given this obstacle it might be better to ski almost exactly 90 degrees *away* from the pole, alongside the pressure ridge, to see if there was a better option. Looking left and right, the pressure ridge didn't seem to change. For all I knew, it could continue for several miles without getting any less difficult— and might even get worse.

We turned right and skied along the outlying ice boulders, knowing that we could be wasting precious time skiing for hours out of our way, only to find ourselves in no better situation. All eyes were focused intently on the wall of debris to our left, scanning for any sign of a possible way through. Every thirty minutes we'd take turns leaving the line and scout a little closer, but separating the team, even if only briefly, made me nervous. All the while, the ticking clock of the drift beneath our skis was getting harder to ignore. As we came ever closer to the pole, the movement of the ice became more significant and more challenging to our navigation.

At this stage, the risk of the drifting ice carrying us away from, or even over, the pole was a distinct possibility. *By accident* was not the way we wanted to arrive at the top of the world. Neither did we want to be carried past it. After an agonizing few hours of skiing, Olga and I scouted the ridge. I had come to trust Olga's judgment completely. We had a lot in common, both of us having instigated and led our own expedition projects in the past. I was sorry that the language barrier seemed to impact Olga's confidence within the team, but when it was just the two of us, it didn't matter. We worked together efficiently and companionably, and I was grateful for the quiet support Olga offered at every opportunity, seemingly able to appreciate in a way that the others perhaps couldn't the pressure of making decisions for the team.

After exploring the outer reaches of the frightening accumulation of ice, we thought we could discern a possible course through the pressure ridge. The traverse looked more challenging than anything we had attempted previously, but better than what lay on either side of it. As we skied back to the group I weighed the risk of trying this route versus the risk of continuing on in the hope of something better. Glancing at Olga as I reported back to the team, she gave me a nod of agreement. This was our shot.

Stuffing snacks into mouths and organizing spare gloves and equipment in readiness for what was to come, we stood in a huddle and made a plan. We would advance into the pressure ridge bit by bit, forming a chain and transferring both people and equipment from one safe spot to the next in a series of short hops, moving together as a group to tackle one stretch at a time for as long as it would take. The deeper we advanced into the pressure ridge, the more we were committed. If it turned out that the route was impassable, we'd have to work our way out of the ridge the same way we'd come in—losing yet more precious hours.

As we progressed ever farther into the rubble, my nerves tightened with the fear that I had made a terrible decision. The team around me were working at their maximum capacity, each finding a role that suited their strength: Heaving the dead weight of the sledges over shoulder-high blockages or finding slithers of space between the shards that were standing tall all around us or gathering ski poles and skis into bundles to ferry them forward using quicker, more demanding shortcuts. I watched in admiration as Asma bustled to and fro, marking out the critical hazards of a section we were traversing—and at one stage lying prone on a slab so that she could repeatedly guide the boots of her teammates into an easily overlooked foothold as they passed, busy wrestling their sledges over a demanding obstacle. Our group effort to cross the pressure ridge was a triumph of teamwork that, even as we toiled, gave me a euphoric buzz of pride. Succeed or fail, we were proving our worth.

Spending a solitary ninety minutes keeping watch for polar bears became thought of as a treat rather than a chore.

After five hours or so of relentless effort, we remained enclosed on all sides by the densely packed wreckage of insanely unnavigable ice. I asked Olga if she could find somewhere to get a forward view, then watched anxiously as she scrambled up a nearby stack. Between heaves at a stubbornly wedged sledge, I stared at her back, trying to glean any hint from her body language of what she could see from her elevated vantage point. She turned and caught my eye, then broke into a grin, raising her fists in the air to pump at the sky. It was good news. In the distance she had been able to see flatter ice beyond the far side of the ridge, and sure enough within an hour we had spilled out of the icy maze of chaos and onto the smooth surface of a perfect ice floe.

As the last sledge, ski pole, and boot were accounted for, we all celebrated with a generous snack break, sitting on our sledges chomping handfuls of food and draining hot drinks from our flasks as the stress of the last six hours dissipated in a moment of shared laughter. There was an upwelling of camaraderie and an emotional glut of confidence and joy. For a few moments the North Pole didn't matter because we were reveling in what we had just achieved and the vindication of so much that it represented. Now, for the first time, not only did we believe we would achieve our goal, we also believed that we deserved it. Finally, we felt worthy.

SUSAN: *The first and last thing we had to do each day we were on the ice was to spit into a tube—for science. It was part of the data collection we were doing for Audrey's POWER study. It took a surprising amount of practice to be able to spit cleanly into a tube the width of a finger, but worse was having to chew absorbent cotton wool for ten minutes the moment we woke up to soak up yet more saliva. The cotton padding would squeak on my teeth and leave my mouth uncomfortably dry.*

Every three days we had to spit into tubes throughout the day in addition to the morning and evening samples. This was challenging. We had to have the right tube on hand, as each was labeled with a specific day and time. Then we had to hold the tiny tube in our enormous mitts and expose our mouth to those punishing temperatures. It sometimes took a moment to muster enough saliva in our mouths to be able to spit. Of course, if your aim was not good, there was no second chance, as the saliva froze almost on contact with the air. Worst of all, this procedure had to be squeezed into the seven-minute breaks we were allowed between ski legs. This was our precious time for drinking, eating, or having a pee. I hated having to nag everyone to follow the protocols, especially on bad days when we were colder, more tired, or struggling to ski over rough ice. I guess this is why there are so few studies carried out on polar expeditions—when your priority is to stay alive, collecting scientific samples seems unimportant.

One night I dreamed I was floating on ice, locked in, cold, far away from safety. As I struggled to wake, I thought I was in Iceland, on the training expedition. Soon I'll be back in the city sleeping in a bed, I *reassured myself, then opened my eyes and remembered where I was—squeezed between Olga and Lamees, both asleep. My heart sank as I lifted myself out of my sleeping bag. I quickly put on my warm jacket and boots and slipped noiselessly out of the tent. I could still hardly breathe and felt scared. Turning around on the spot I counted our three tents under the Arctic summer sun. I was floating on ice. My nightmare was real. We were on our way to the North Pole.*

I spotted Nataša walking peacefully around the camp and could hear the sound of her feet stepping on the ice. She was on polar bear watch. I don't know if it was watching her steady pace that calmed me, but I started breathing deeper and easier. My heart slowed and I smiled. Yes, I reminded myself, I might be cold and standing on drifting ice in the middle of nowhere, but I was on my way to reach a dream and that felt good.

We were true explorers. I was overwhelmed by love as I thought of family, friends, and all the people who had supported me throughout my journey. None of us would have been there without the support and love of those closest to us back home. Throughout the previous two years, they had trusted us and encouraged us. I also thought a lot about those Arctic guides in Longyearbyen who had doubted our team. I could see now that they had made their judgment without knowing anything about us. They hadn't witnessed us buried in the snow during the storm in Iceland, or taking turns to heave sledges one at a time up precipitous dunes in the heat of Oman, or repeatedly rehearsing lighting the stoves until we could do it with our eyes closed. They had no idea what we were capable of as individuals or as a team and had been wrong to underestimate us. We were well prepared and we were determined.

It was only now, as we were making our journey, that we were discovering for ourselves just how *well prepared. No one on the team fit the image of a polar explorer that I had previously carried in my mind, reinforced by history and the polar veterans we had met. None of us had the look of the polar guides in Longyearbyen. But here we were in our still-too-new clothes, skiing to the North Pole regardless. The women sleeping in the tents all around me were just as much polar explorers as any guide who had skied to the North Pole a hundred times.*

Everything is hard on the ice. When you are cold all day, sore from pulling a sledge and tired from little sleep, the smallest task feels impossible. When the opportunity finally comes to sit in your corner of the tent at the end of a long day, you don't get to relax. Sharing a small space with three other team members who are equally tired means that you are never really comfortable. My corner of the tent was closest to the kitchen. When my grandmother learned I was in charge of the tent kitchen she gave me her apron to take with me. It was one of the few nonessential items Felicity allowed me to take. My grandmother was worried about how well we would eat in those harsh conditions, and I'm not sure my attempts to describe our gastronomic routine did much to alleviate her concerns.

Every morning and evening, I lit up the stove in the tent kitchen. Once lit, it needed constant attention to prevent a fire, which would be deadly on the pack ice, so far from alternative shelter. The stove was alight for hours every day, constantly melting snow and ice to replenish all the flasks, to rehydrate our food rations for breakfast and dinner, to fill up our hot water bottles, and to warm our sleeping bags when we slept. It was a seemingly endless job involving intensely watching big chunks of packed snow melt into disappointingly small pools of water. This constant cycle of adding the snow and melting it down for hours every day, day after day, while making sure the tent didn't burn, wore me down. I would look at Steph, Lamees, and Olga, sitting in the other corners of the tent, and I would dream of sitting in their place, far from the stove that was enslaving me. It became a fixation, and over time I hated more and more my corner of the tent. It felt like a prison that prevented me from switching off, even for just a couple of minutes.

My kitchen resentment built up. One morning Steph and Lamees both disappeared just when we needed to collapse the tent and depart for the day. Breaking camp was normally a tight routine and synchronized between all the tents—fifteen minutes of coordinated tasks carried out in a specific order to make sure everything was packed safely and everyone was ready to ski at the same time. Half my tent team had decided it was the right moment for a prolonged toilet break. I lost my temper and couldn't just sit waiting for them. I piled up all their stuff outside the tent on the ice. This felt like a minirevolution to express my feelings. Steph and Lamees, both knowing me well by this stage, smiled and said nothing when they came back from their ablutions—but made sure from then on to be ready on time.

Felicity checked on all of us each evening, to share any important news and let us know the departure time for the following morning.

She was usually our only visitor, as everyone else was too exhausted or too busy to pop in on their neighbors. But one evening Misba squeezed into our tent and chatted away for nearly an hour. Mama Misba, as we called her, was the oldest team member. She was our hero, a kind mother and soon-to-be grandmother who always looked out for everyone else. She had never skied before meeting Felicity and yet she was now on her way to the North Pole.

Like me, Misba was in charge of her tent's kitchen, and she too was fed up with her duties. She was first up in the cold every morning and continued melting ice until late at night to replenish all the containers and prepare bedtime hot chocolate for her tent-mates. The more Misba talked, the better I felt. I wasn't alone anymore. We understood each other. When Misba left, Olga, Lamees, and Steph looked at me and thanked me for the great job I was doing in the kitchen. From then on, they made sure to acknowledge with big smiles how wonderful the food was or how perfect was the temperature of their hot water bottle.

MISBA: *We had soon settled into a routine. Our extensive training now paid dividends, for our camp drill was slick, and I knew my own role back to front. I would rise at seven, moving quickly to get warm, and deflate two of the sleeping mats to make room for the stove. Then I would start the stove and heat the water from the plastic water flask I had used as a hot water bottle the night before. Once hot, I'd use that water to make porridge. Nobody talked in the mornings because we were all moving so quickly to start the day. While the team was eating porridge, I made hot chocolate and distributed the prepared bags of snacks for the day from the expedition rations. Then I heated more water to fill everyone's water bottles and flasks for the day. Ida would leave the tent, followed by Asma and Anisa, while I packed and cleared the kitchen, brushed the tent, put on my boots, and zipped the door closed. At nine o'clock it was time to take down the tents, put on*

skis and harnesses, pop a couple of hand warmers in my mitts, clip the sledges to the harnesses—and off we went.

At the end of each day we reversed the routine. As soon as the tent took shape I was first inside. Asma threw in our sleeping bags and foam sleeping mats while I unpacked the kitchen and set to work preparing a four-course meal complete with two cups of hot chocolate. During training, my stove skills had been shaky, but now I was superconfident. Asma had bought a fire blanket to keep close to the stove in the tent kitchen, but it was never needed. I had no accidents during the expedition nor did I cry for help once. I was an expert! I was surprised not to have any issues, but it demonstrated how superb the training had been, and I saw that the practice I had done at home had been worth it.

At mealtimes, I started melting blocks of snow for water and announced to the team what was for dinner. Each day there was a different variety of freeze-dried rice or pasta with meat or pulses. Macaroni and cheese was my favorite. We even had freeze-dried desserts, which I didn't like so much. We ate together, spooning the food out of our individual foil bags in which the meals were prepared, while wet clothes and socks hung from the washing line we had stretched across the roof of the inner tent. As they began to dry, the clothes would steam and smell. Though I found the tent cramped, with little room to shuffle from kitchen space to sleeping area, this was my favorite time, the only time during the whole day I could feel cozy. After skiing for eight or nine hours, I just wanted to eat and sit beside the burner. The heat from the stove was heaven.

After our meal, everyone focused on making sure their own clothing was as dry as possible for the next day. It was a time-consuming job with only two small stoves to provide any heat. I also made a second round of hot drinks for everyone. I got to know how everyone liked theirs. Asma and Anisa liked to mix hot chocolate and coffee together—

Susan enjoying a rehydrated meal in the tent

calling it a mocha! Occasionally I would ask someone to look after the stoves so that I could go outside, but the toilet drill was not easy. Mitts, jacket, hats, and boots would all have to be put on before exiting the tent, and coming back into the tent again was a nightmare. You were not popular if you let snow into the tent as you returned. In most cases I was scolded for bringing in snow all over my jacket.

Despite the cramped and often awkward conditions, the tent quickly became home for me, as I refused to think of my home in Manchester while on the expedition. Previous adventures had taught me that thinking of family or my usual life made it difficult for me to enjoy the moment I was experiencing and absorb the impact of the place and the people around me. While tending the stove in our tent, I often thought of the sea just beneath me. There were always things to make me reflect on nature's power, putting my own experiences into perspective. These thoughts motivated me to pray and ask God for a safe journey.

In preparing mentally for the expedition I had relied on my faith, which is central to everything I do. It governs my values; lifestyle; relationships with family and friends; and mental, emotional, and spiritual well-being. While some people use yoga to rejuvenate the body and mind, for me, as a Muslim, daily prayers are as important as physical training. Prayer enhances my concentration and reduces stress.

Praying on time is paramount for people of the Muslim faith, as is knowing the qibla, *the direction of prayer. The direction must be toward Makkah, the religious city of primary importance to Islam which is located in modern-day Saudi Arabia. At home this is straightforward, but in unfamiliar locations it can be very challenging to determine the right direction. Normally Muslims must pray at five specific times during the day, but I was able to combine midday and afternoon prayers. This meant I could pray in the morning before I left the tent, in the evening in the tent before sleeping, and just once while out in the open skiing.*

Misba (left) and Lamees checking on each other during a brief break in the skiing across the Arctic Ocean

For me the purpose of prayer is to bring myself in touch with God. Just as the body has physical needs such as food and water, the soul has needs, too. Praying out in spectacular nature, I had the opportunity to reflect on the beauty of vast ice sheets glittering in the sun.

When praying I normally wear a jubba, a long tunic covering that falls to my feet, as well as a head covering. On expedition I used a hat or a scarf to cover my head and had to make other adjustments, too.

Prior to prayer there is a ritual called wudu, *which involves cleaning parts of the body such as face, hands, and arms. Without easy access to water on our expedition I did dry* wudu, *using elements of the earth such as snow and ice.*

Some of the older members of my community back home had been concerned that I would miss prayers and be unable to perform the ablutions before praying. It was just one way in which they saw outdoor life to be incompatible with Islam. I don't see that there is any restriction at all. To be outdoors as we reflect can put our lives into perspective. It's an opportunity to consider our values and existence on this earth. Our religion encourages all of this. Rather than resent the negative response from some to my participation in the expedition, I decided to welcome it. The way I saw it, in giving them answers to their questions I was creating a positive dialogue that might help change some attitudes.

In the past I had worked as a hospital chaplain and enjoyed it very much, especially moving around the wards visiting patients. I thought I'd try something similar on the team. A few days into the expedition, I visited the other team tents. I went to Felicity and Nataša first and found an immaculately clean and spacious tent that was so roasting hot I thought I was in the tropics. Felicity showed me a simple map of our journey so far, just little dots indicating where we had camped each day, and how close we were to the North Pole. Thinking of my own struggles with map reading, I wondered why all maps couldn't be that easy. Nataša seized on my visit as an opportunity to record a podcast. We sat together in the tent talking as she recorded, but I was slightly distracted by the fact that I had brought my mug with me, expecting to be offered a cup of tea when I visited. But no offer!

Hospitality clearly doesn't exist at the North Pole, I said to myself as I took my dry mug to the next tent. There I found Susan and Olga having a face-cleaning session but was shocked to discover that Susan had already closed her kitchen for the night. "I have strict rules. My kitchen closes at eight-thirty sharp every night," she explained. "If anyone has missed dinner or wants a hot drink after that—tough," she added with a shrug. When I described the contrasting situation in our tent, that I prepared whatever my tent-mates wanted until they chose to go to bed and was often the last up clearing the kitchen and doing the washing, it was Susan's turn to be shocked.

"There's no way I am cleaning anyone's things," she said, "especially if they give them to me after the kitchen is closed."

I returned to my tent thoughtful—and still without a cup of tea.

IDA: *During the first Iceland training, I had been really pleased when Felicity told us the tent groups she had put together. I had already naturally gravitated toward Anisa as someone I could work with well. She was efficient, thorough, and cheerful. I had also been instinctively drawn to Misba. She had an amazing way of recognizing everyone's needs. I had not yet spent much time with Asma, and my first impression was that it could be a challenge to have her on our tent team. I'd noticed that she tended to ignore advice in favor of her own intuition. But I was determined that, no matter what, we four were going to become a tight group who would support and help each other.*

We soon decided together the roles we would each have in the tent. Misba wanted to be the indoor person in charge of the stove and cooking. Asma was going to be her support in the kitchen after taking in all the equipment to the tent from our sledges. Anisa and I were to be the outside persons, which meant that we would be last inside the tents and first up in the mornings. It would be up to us to secure the tent. If more snow was needed for melting, I would go out to fetch it; if fuel for the stoves was needed, I would go out to refill the fuel bottles. Cleaning the dishes was also something Anisa and I took care of, as Misba and Asma had already prepared the food. With everything decided, everyone

felt happy with the team structure, each of us doing the roles we liked best, and we were feeling confident that we could cope with whatever the expedition threw at us.

However, everything had changed during the first days of the expedition. Asma had struggled a lot with her skis and boots. The straps of the bindings that tied her boots to the skis kept coming undone. Several times I helped her tighten the fastenings, but every time they would slowly work loose again. I could see that she was trying hard not to let it get her down, but over time she was losing strength as she attempted to ski in ways that wouldn't cause the bindings to come loose. It was hard to watch.

I'd tried to support her as much as possible in those first few days. I'd been worried about Asma being a part of my tent team, but she showed herself to be far stronger than I expected. Despite the problems with her skis, she stepped up and revealed a whole new character. Each evening after she had finished her job of putting all the equipment and bags from the sledges into the tent, she wouldn't go inside to the warmth of the shelter right away but would instead help me finish off securing the tent. She had an amazing way of simply asking what she could do and then getting on with it without any fuss. We worked really well together, and I felt so proud of her as a tent-mate. All my concerns about her vanished, and I was happy to have been proved so wrong.

Ironically, it was those who had seemed so confident during training that appeared to struggle the most. During the training expeditions, it was obvious that Anisa was the fittest of us all, and I didn't have the slightest worry about her skiing to the North Pole. But out on the ice something changed. On the very first day she had been very tired and complained of pain. Everyone was tired that first day, and I assumed

Asma sitting on her sledge during a ski break. The tape on her face is to protect her skin from cold injury and the wind.

the pain was her body adjusting to the cold or to the effect on new muscles of the skiing and clambering over ice. But it didn't get better. Anisa and I were supposed to be the last ones to get into the tent at the end of each day, but this became very hard for Anisa. Similarly in the mornings, Anisa and I were supposed to be the first ones out of the tent, but she struggled to find her gear and sort herself out. It became clear that looking after herself was about the most she could do. The strongest woman had become the one who needed the most help. And vice versa: it was Asma who would come outside to help me instead.

Long days hauling a heavy sledge, alone with your own thoughts for hours while you ski, being tired and hungry and faced with the possibility that perhaps you are not as invincible as you thought, can very quickly change a person. As Asma increasingly stepped in for Anisa, all the melting of snow to make drinking water for the next day and all the cooking fell on Misba. I know this became hard on her.

What none of us had anticipated was that it wasn't just the demands of the ice that was hard, it was also being part of such a complex team. None of us knows for sure exactly how we will respond to feeling out of our depth—until we have experienced it. The journey to the North Pole is all about high ice and hard truth.

Learning something afresh rather than having to let go of an ingrained attitude is often easier. I knew myself how hard it was to give up the comfort of familiar ways of doing things, of long-held preferences, how difficult it can be to place trust in a new method or in someone else's system in the hope it is a positive change. During our time in the desert, I had learned more about the strengths, behaviors, skills, and experience of each member of the team. I had learned how, when this kaleidoscope of differences is put together, it creates a whole that is much stronger, much greater than the sum of its parts. The inspiration I drew from my teammates was the importance of not only believing in yourself but also believing in others. I realized that, while the goal was important to me, what was also important was the feeling of working together to reach that goal. It was the team that would make reaching the North Pole possible—or not—so we needed to help each other as best we could and figure out what we could each do to help us get to the top of the world…together.

The last leg to the top of the world

TWELVE

Our North Pole

You don't so much conquer the North Pole as stalk it. The team crowded close behind me as I held out my GPS and counted off the strides. We were less than a hundred yards away. As a rule, handheld GPS devices like those we were using are only accurate to a few yards, and as you get closer to a spot location they become wildly erratic. The numbers on my GPS began jumping around so much that it eventually rendered the device useless. At ten yards distance I put it away, trusting that ten generous strides would bring us accurately enough to the top of the world. With a whoop, I plunged my ski poles into the snow after the tenth pace. "The North Pole!" I cheered. The team erupted into celebration.

There were hugs and tears, laughing and expressions of relief. Anisa dropped to her knees to pray, while others stepped away for a private moment to do the same. Ida pulled out her GPS to photograph its display registering 90.000, and for some time she was striding around the floe as the numbers twitched uncooperatively. Inspired, several others followed suit and before long team members were scattered across the sea ice, each finding their very own North Pole.

I returned to my ski poles, still standing where I had placed them on arrival, now surrounded by a blast pattern of hastily discarded skis and

The exact point of 90N—and a passing snowflake—captured perfectly

sledges. They had only marked the North Pole for the briefest of moments. The ice that held them had already been shifted by wind and
current over the point of 90 degrees north. The top of the world was
probably already a few strides distant. Years ago, in a school physics
class, I learned that it is impossible for two people ever to see the same
rainbow, even if they are standing right next to each other. I treasure
that fact every time I see a rainbow, knowing that only I can see this
exact shimmering phenomenon. I got the same pleasure from knowing

that this precise spot on an anonymous ice floe in the Arctic Ocean would never again be the North Pole. It would forever be our North Pole and only our North Pole. I liked that. It felt fitting that we'd never have to share it. So much about this journey was unique and would only be known and understood by those women who stood with me. It was a shared experience that I knew for the rest of our lives would bind us—a bond quite unlike any other.

The blast pattern of hastily discarded skis and sledges. The upright ski poles on the left mark the position of the North Pole on our arrival.

IDA: *We were eight miles away from the top of the world. Everywhere was cold, sharp, and bright. Once again I looked at my GPS. While sleeping we had drifted more than three miles to the west and over a half-mile to the north. That meant a half-mile closer to the North Pole.*

The ice seemed to be drifting faster the closer we got to 90 degrees north. Would today be the day we would make it to the northernmost spot on the planet? The ice ahead looked like a pristine plain of white. We might be lucky, I thought. Maybe it would stay as flat all the way. We set off into skiing heaven, the unspoken question in everyone's mind—would this be the day? The climbing, skiing, pulling, and bear watches of the past days all melted together, but each memory hung in the air as we slowly pulled our still-heavy sledges. Memories from home crowded my mind, too. Recollecting these moments of happiness gave me strength and kept me pushing forward. I plugged the headphones from my MP3 player in my ears and let the music give wings to my mind, my imagination lending new life and interest to the white surroundings.

At 6:00 p.m., I saw the crossed poles raised overhead at the front of the line. This was usually the signal that we were stopping for the day to pitch the tents. Not today. Felicity gathered the team and gave us a choice: "If we carry on we might make it today. Or we can camp now and make it tomorrow."

I looked back at the plain we had crossed and could see our ski tracks trailing southward. We had covered a considerable distance, but there was still two miles to go. We were tired, weak, and sore. It was tempting to set up camp immediately and ski the last leg the following day, when we would have the energy to enjoy the celebration of our arrival. On the other hand, the pack ice on which we rested might drift. Every day the drift swept us farther west, and we feared being carried past the pole and having to fight against the movement of the ice to ski back. There was also the worry of what unforeseen conditions and challenges we would face if we waited until tomorrow.

So for me there was no contest. "Let's carry on," urged Misba, reading my mind. Eventually this became the majority verdict. "Right," said Felicity, "let's find the North Pole!" We all waved our poles in the air with joy. Yet the realization that we were about to reach the geographic North Pole, 90 degrees north, the top of the world, was hard to grab hold of. We had been fighting so hard,

Ida pausing to admire the view just hours from the North Pole

Team celebrations at the North Pole complete with the film crew and production guides

particularly during that last day, that it was a shock to think it might soon be over.

There were lots of tears during that last two miles. For some it was because we had finally made it to our destination, a moment of victory. But for me, I was sad because it was a moment of loss, a journey come to an end. For almost three years we had been a team reaching for the same goal, despite being women with such different backgrounds of various religions and cultures, facing our individual struggles and discovering our own motivations. But now the tears and the GPS were telling me it was almost over. I didn't want that. Together we had reached our frozen dream and I wanted it to keep going on, to reach more goals. I wanted us to go on until we had convinced the whole world that it is possible to reach your dreams, no matter how big, distant, and unlikely they might be. We were proof.

SUSAN: *Everyone was exhausted from the excruciating efforts of the previous days, but we were getting near our goal. Felicity spent the day cheering the women behind, trying to keep the spirits up for those that were struggling the most, while Olga and I did our best to identify the most suitable route and constantly adapt the pace to the mood. The final day was a hard day, but even though we couldn't really see each other's faces when protected from the cold, we could still feel the smiles all around. This incredible moment that we had been dreaming of for the last two years was happening.*

I recalled the first time I had met all the women in Reykjavik Airport before our first training expedition. I remembered how skeptical I had been that any of us were capable of skiing to the North Pole—and the thought made me smile. Back then I had wondered how we were going to greet each other: a kiss on both cheeks comme les français? *A British hug? Something more reserved? In the end it turned out to be a simple handshake. Now, as we approached the climax of our journey, I smiled to myself, thinking how different it would be when we would all have to say good-bye.*

OLGA: *Before the expedition and every day during it, I had imagined in vivid detail the moment we would reach the North Pole. I had* *imagined elation, tears of joy, and euphoria. When the moment came and we finally reached the top of the world, I didn't feel any of that. I felt happy, of course, that we had achieved our goal but also sad that this big adventure had ended so soon. Despite having counted miles and hours, degrees and days, the end seemed to have crept up on me and arrived suddenly. I couldn't tell you whether it was happiness or sadness that was the stronger emotion as we neared our destination.*

It was a gloomy day. Everything around us was gray. The white snow merged with the off-white sky, shrouding our surroundings as if the whole world was shrinking back into invisibility. The dense white haze was very tiring, as it was impossible to tell whether we were walking up or down. Sometimes it would seem to me that there was a slight lump ahead but when I put my leg up to step on it, I would instead fall into a small pit. My eyes began to hurt from stress and the pressure of trying to see where, and how, to move forward.

A half-mile from the pole we stopped for our last break. We straightened our clothes, making sure the national flags sewn at our shoulders and the sponsor logos on our chests were clearly visible, and wiped our faces to the best extent possible, knowing that there was a special moment ahead. One last pressure ridge stood in our way. As before, we formed a line to help each other drag sledges, skis, and poles over the ice rubble. Everyone was in high spirits because the pole was so near. Someone called out every time we counted off another hundred yards. At the final hundred yards, the whole team stood next to each other, shoulder to shoulder, forming a single horizontal line. We skied forward together, each holding our own GPS unit and counting down: thirty yards, twenty yards, ten….

"North Pole!" Felicity shouted as she stuck a ski pole in the snow to mark the exact location of 90 degrees north.

The North Pole is not a specific point on the map. There is no ceremonial marker out there on the ice to mark the intersection of

Earth's axes. There is nothing to see when you reach 90 degrees north except ice and snow that look the same as every other patch of ice and snow for hundreds of miles in every direction. The North Pole does not exist on its own; what exists is the meaning we bring to this unique geographical point. The North Pole, I learned, is built upon our dreams and our imagination.

The team posing for a celebratory photograph on a lump of ice close to the
North Pole with their individual national flags

THIRTEEN
On Top of the World

The helicopter that came to collect us from the pole and return us to Barneo brought with it a very special passenger. I don't think we realized how incomplete we felt without Mariam until she was back with us. Her hands were heavily wrapped in protective mitts to keep them warm, and I wouldn't hear the details of her injury or her time alone in Barneo for some time to come, but I immediately read in her face the difficulty of the previous week and was fearful for her. Stepping off the helicopter, she was enveloped in down-jacketed hugs from the rest of the team, a charge led, of course, by Nataša. Even though Mariam's recovery would be a long process, I hoped the outpouring of affection during this unique reunion at the top of the world might mark the start of her journey toward healing.

We posed together for photographs at the North Pole as a complete team, including the film crew and their guides. It is an image I knew I would treasure for the memories it represented but also for the inspiration it would carry to so many. Anisa was now the first Omani to have skied to the North Pole; Lamees was the first woman from Kuwait to have skied to the North Pole; Steph was the first Cypriot to ski to the North Pole (and simultaneously the first to have skied to both North and South geographic poles); Asma was the first Qatari to ski to the

North Pole; and Misba was the first British Muslim to ski to the North Pole. Those records not only sent a strong and positive message that the team would carry home with them to their respective countries; they also formed a platform from which each woman could share her stories and experiences. It made them effective ambassadors both for their gender and the Arctic. The rest of us on the team may not have been returning with records, but we still had a role to play in engaging others and realizing the central purposes of our expedition. In that respect, our journey was not over. There was plenty of work yet to be done.

As the helicopter flew us back to Barneo, a journalist who had accompanied the flight to report on our story sat next to me and handed me a headset so we could speak.

"I came here to report on a joke," he told me.

He was a correspondent for a Russian newspaper, but as an Arabist he had lived in the Middle East for many years. He described how, when he was told that women from the Gulf region were attempting to ski to the North Pole, he had dismissed it as an amusing impossibility, a likely story of failure that would raise a knowing laugh.

"I see now that I was wrong," he said looking at the newly seasoned polar explorers who filled the helicopter. "I wanted you to know that this expedition has changed what I believe about women, and Arabic women in particular. I am going to write about that."

I nodded my thanks for his frankness but couldn't speak. On the one hand I was glad that the expedition was already changing perceptions, as I'd hoped it would. But on the other, it was demoralizing to know that there was still so much misconception out there that needed changing. The belief that women are somehow "less" is one still held by many, whether consciously or not, in a way that affects our societies, our cultures, and the lives of us all, every single day. As we move into a new decade of a still-new century, the majority of women across Europe and the Middle East are still fighting against obstacles that prevent them having proper control over their own lives, whether it is the system of male guardianship that persists in the Middle East, or the abortion laws in Europe decided by male-majority offices, or the lack of representation in politics and boardrooms that remains globally endemic.

I find it hard to accept that these injustices remain the case in my own lifetime. As a woman who has been fortunate to have both freedom and privilege, I feel a sense of responsibility. My lifetime is, after all, my watch. Even within my own specialization I notice small details that are often dismissed as unimportant and yet are part of the systemic reinforcement of an ingrained prejudice that needs to be weeded out. I see it everywhere: on the shelves of the "adventure" section of bookstores, where all the books are about male explorers by male authors; in the ad for a heavily promoted speaking event on the theme of endurance, with a completely male (and completely white) lineup; in the prime-time TV show billed as capturing a real "expedition" during which only men are seen on camera. These instances of everyday sexism add up to a devastating message that is being transmitted to the next generation as well as my own.

I gazed down from the helicopter at the frozen Arctic, crazed with leads and pressure ridges, just as I had at the start of the expedition. I remembered how I had felt standing on the ice surveying those ridges, which seemed impossible to cross, how the scale of the task seemed to paralyze my ability to act. There was a parallel to be drawn with the global problems we are facing—social justice and environmental change—which are issues of such scale and complexity that action feels hopeless and we individuals, powerless.

Yet if we have the courage to commit to the task, even when the route ahead and the end are unclear, we can make a difference and we can succeed. When facing those pressure ridges, which had so vividly highlighted our shortcomings and weaknesses as a team, rather than giving up, everyone had instead found a way to contribute that drew on their personal strengths. As a result, what should have been the worst of times was transformed into a moment of triumph. The memory of them left me inspired. This was the message we needed to share with the world.

LAMEES: *During our time on the ice, I think I surprised a lot of people. A few days into the journey, I was skiing alongside another teammate, who said teasingly, "I wonder what happened to Lamees? She is so focused and alert to everything that is happening around her!" I knew that the expedition experience was making me a better person, but it is extra rewarding when other people notice.*

One day I was skiing alongside Misba. She was talking to me as we skied about how hard she had found the expedition. "How are we going to survive this?" she asked me.

I shared with her my newfound secret. "Thoughts become things," I told her. "Every minute that passes is a moment we will not get back. We have to be sure to keep ourselves thinking positively until the very last moment. Otherwise we will regret it and never get this opportunity again."

I could see that Misba was surprised to hear me say such things. I don't think she expected it of me. She told me later that she had remembered my words and that they had helped her through the days and the difficulties that were to come.

Felicity, too, found an opportunity to talk to me privately one day. "You are the youngest on the team, and I was really worried about how you would cope out here," she told me. "But you have proved me wrong. You are doing great and I'm very proud of you."

We are all shaped by the experiences of our lives, and when looking back on those years as part of the team, I wouldn't change a minute. I signed up for the expedition not knowing what I was getting myself into, but I praise the moment of taking that risk to jump into the unknown. I gained some beloved and exceptional friends and learned that one of the most vital lessons in life is to stick with your team. I also gained confidence in my ability to be a role model to all women, to show them that despite all the hardship, we can adapt to what is new and unfamiliar. Set up a goal, aim at it, put your mind and heart into it, and you will be able to reach anywhere you want to in life. I believe that now more than ever before.

The message on the back of Susan's sledge that helped everyone on the team keep going

Mariam (left) and Misba on the helicopter back to Barneo, having been reunited at the North Pole

MARIAM: *My team reached the North Pole. Those last hours, as I waited to be reunited with them, were the longest of my life. But it was well worth the wait. I stepped off the helicopter with tears already running down my face. No one except Felicity had any idea that I was coming, and the look of surprise on the faces of the team was priceless. I saw Asma first and watched her eyes well with tears. The love I felt as the team wrapped me in hugs was just perfect. I was so proud of them all for making it to the North Pole.*

We all expressed how happy we were at that moment, and it felt like a victorious reunion. Filled with so much joy, it was emotionally overwhelming. After all the hugs, Nataša pulled me aside, where she handed me my national flag from her pocket.

"Hold it up so that I can take your picture," she urged me. I held up the flag and started crying again. I was here. I had made it.

What does it mean to reach the North Pole? The landscape is the same for miles. If it weren't for the GPS stating that you are standing at 90 degrees north, you wouldn't even know you've reached it. You're standing on the most northern point on Earth, and everything from that point is south. You could say you're on top of the world. It is an amazing concept and an exhilarating feeling, but that's not why you take part in such expeditions. We've all heard the saying "It's not about the destination; it's about the journey." I've always liked that idea, but this experience made it a deep-rooted belief. The journey is where the growth happens; where the friendships are made; where the obstacles arise, plans change, personality and attitude are challenged, strength is found, beauty seen, fear faced, vulnerability embraced, wisdom and clarity gained, and—perhaps most importantly—stories created. It's the heart of it all. The destination is simply a way to get you moving, a means to get you truly living and truly looking, inside and out.

History will reveal whether the team will be among the last to ski to the North Pole.

FOURTEEN

#

When asked to address audiences about climate change, I'm wary of dwelling too much on the problems of environmental damage caused by human activity. I don't want to deepen the despondency of those listening—the media has started calling it *climate fatigue*. I may not have the solution to anthropogenic climate change, but in my stories of polar expeditions and polar science, I do have examples of the unmatched brilliance of human beings as a species. We are innovative, ingenious, and persistent. We have found ways to not only survive environments so extreme that they are inconsistent with life, but to explore and understand them. Our development as a species has caused the crisis we currently face, but it has also provided us with the tools and capability to fix it.

In 2000, when I was posted to Rothera Research Station in Antarctica as a meteorologist, one of my main responsibilities was to take ozone measurements, part of a wider monitoring of ozone in the upper atmosphere. Ozone is a gas that forms a natural layer that protects the surface of the earth from harmful ultraviolet radiation emitted by the sun. Without it, life on earth would be very different, if not impossible. During the 1980s, a seasonal thinning of the ozone layer was discovered over Antarctica. Later, it became clear that this ozone "hole" was caused by manufactured chemicals being released into the atmosphere by human industry. It was perhaps the first time the world was faced irrefutably and publicly with the reality that our activity had the ability to disrupt the very mechanics of our environment on a planetary scale, in a way that threatened the existence of all life on Earth. It was a moment of existential as well as environmental epiphany for humankind.

The international community responded with the 1987 Montreal Protocol, which banned the production of ozone-depleting substances. Despite being the most universally ratified and rapidly adopted international agreement ever seen at that time, it was neither an easy nor a quick fix to the problem of the ozone hole. But ultimately it has been a success. Some four decades after it was discovered, seasonal ozone depletion is at its lowest extent since monitoring began and is expected to return to preindustrial levels by the end of the century.

Antarctica provides another important precedent, too. The 1950s are not a decade of history generally celebrated for tolerance and international cooperation, yet in 1959 twelve nations with significant interests in the continent signed the Antarctic Treaty. This inspired agreement neither recognized nor refuted any of the competing sovereignty claims over Antarctica but did set aside the entire continent for peaceful, scientific, international cooperation. In the decades since, more than forty additional nations have signed up to the treaty, and other agreements have been added to the original articles to address specific issues such as environmental protection, the regulation of activity concerning mineral resources, and the conservation of wildlife. The initial agreement has now expanded into the Antarctic Treaty System (ATS), which effectively governs the continent through a unique process of international collaboration. As many who are involved in polar politics would be quick to point out, the ATS is far from perfection. But it is an important and positive example of the nations of the world finding new and lasting solutions. If we have the will.

We know that human civilization has the power and the knowledge to alter the planet. So far, the impact of our activity on Earth has been overwhelmingly to its detriment, but we are capable of learning to use that same ability and our talents as a species to alter our planet for its betterment, and our own too. What is lost is unforgivable, but it could

The Women's Euro-Arabian North Pole Expedition 2018

be worse if we forget that there is still so much to save. Landscapes of change, from the shifting ice ridges of the Arctic Ocean to the metaphorical landscapes of culture and society, can be intimidating. But they can also be exhilarating. It is when we encounter change that we have the opportunity to show the very best of ourselves and to draw on all the years of amassing knowledge, skills, expertise, and the confidence to use them, precisely for the purpose of being able to contend with challenge and difficulty when it comes.

Only when we are put to the test do we know what we are capable of; only in adversity do we find triumph. In facing adversity together on the ice, our expedition gained renewed confidence in themselves, as a group and as individuals, myself included. Periods of change come with fear, doubt, and mistakes, but they are also when we can have the greatest impact. They are an opportunity to shape the future and create lasting legacy. What a privilege that opportunity is. We refer to the era of polar exploration at the turn of the nineteenth century as the heroic age of exploration, but today the stakes are so much higher, perhaps the highest they've ever been in human history. It is no hyperbole to say that our world is in peril. The next century has the potential to be the most heroic we've ever seen.

The message that I hope becomes the legacy of our expedition is that, man or woman, young or old, European or Arabian, we all have a responsibility to be fully engaged in the world we live in and to shape that world. By striving to exceed the expectation of others, however we choose to do that, and perhaps even exceeding our own expectations of ourselves in the process, we can each drive forward progress as individuals and together as one mighty whole. We do it by tackling one metaphorical ice boulder or sea-smoking lead at a time, but we must do it now. *Yalla*!

Team Biographies

NATAŠA BRISKI (Slovenia) started her career as a sports journalist before tackling international politics as a correspondent in Washington, DC, and more recently founding her own media network. She remains one of the most prominent online and broadcast journalists in Slovenia.

SUSAN GALLON (France) is a marine biologist who has completed field seasons on sub-Antarctic islands to study marine mammals. More recently, she has dedicated her expertise to develop marine-protected areas. Susan was instrumental in establishing the scientific work undertaken by the expedition and is an active ambassador for STEM, particularly for women and young people.

MARIAM HAMEEDALDIN (Saudi Arabia) is the founder of Humming Tree, a co-working space and community center that hosts entrepreneurs and facilitates events that foster genuine expression and collaboration. Through this space and her daytime job as an instructional coach for an educational tech company, she helps individuals achieve their interpersonal and professional development goals

LAMEES NIJEM (Kuwait) is a motion graphics designer and keen runner. She is the first person from Kuwait to ski to the North Pole and was a winner at the Arab Woman of the Year awards in 2019.

MISBA KHAN (UK) is a financial officer for the National Health Service in the UK as well as a volunteer chaplain at her local hospital. She is the first British Muslim woman to ski to the North Pole and has since been in huge demand to share her experiences with groups within the British Muslim community and beyond. She has climbed several international peaks and continues her mountaineering journey.

IDA OLSSON (Sweden) is a kayak master, polar bear guard, and leader on expedition vessels exploring the Arctic and Antarctic. She also leads snowmobile tours to see polar bears in Svalbard, where she remains a resident.

ANISA AL-RAISSI (Oman) is an outdoor activity instructor with Outward Bound Oman in Muscat. She became the first person from Oman to ski to the North Pole and continues to facilitate personal development journeys for young people in Oman and beyond.

OLGA RUMYANTSEVA (Russia) is a mountaineer instructor and tour guide who had previously climbed the highest volcano on each continent as well as completing many other physical challenges. She works for the biggest adventure tour operator in Russia and is much in demand as a tour leader, sharing her polar experiences with all her guests to encourage them to cultivate their own ambitions.

STEPHANIE SOLOMONIDES (Cyprus) works in an investment bank and, having made pioneering expeditions to both ends of the world, is the first person from Cyprus to ski to the North Pole and the South Pole.

ASMA AL-THANI (Qatar) is a marketing director with the Qatar Olympic Committee and the first woman from Qatar to ski to the North Pole. Previously she was also part of the first women's team from Qatar to climb Mt. Kilimanjaro, and she is now embarking on an ambitious mountaineering campaign to climb some of the world's most coveted peaks.

Time Line

1909	First claim to have reached the geographic North Pole over the surface of the Arctic Ocean with dogs (disputed)
1911	First expedition to reach the geographic South Pole
1969	First undisputed claim to reach the geographic North Pole over the surface of the Arctic Ocean (with dogs and airdrops)
1979	Satellite monitoring of Arctic Ocean sea ice begins.
1986	First woman to reach the geographic North Pole (with dogs)
1994	First person to ski solo and unsupported to the geographic North Pole

1994	Barneo camp established at the North Pole for the first time
2000	Felicity Aston begins a three-year post on the British Antarctic base, Rothera Research Station.
2002	First all-women team to ski to the geographic North Pole
2009	Felicity Aston leads an international team of women on skis to the geographic South Pole.
2012	Felicity Aston becomes the first woman to ski across Antarctica.
JANUARY 2016	Recruitment efforts begin for the Women's Euro-Arabian North Pole Expedition.
SEPTEMBER 2016	First team training expedition in Iceland
FEBRUARY 2017	Team training expedition in Oman
2018	National Oceanic and Atmospheric Administration (NOAA) estimates that 85 percent of multiyear ice in the Arctic Ocean has disappeared.

FEBRUARY 2018	Second team training expedition in Iceland
LATE MARCH 2018	Expedition team arrive in Longyearbyen, Svalbard
APRIL 15, 2018	Day One of the expedition. The team members depart Longyearbyen for Barneo on the Arctic Ocean and are transferred to the start point of the expedition.
APRIL 16, 2018	Emergency evacuation of Mariam to Barneo
APRIL 21, 2018, 6:43 PM	The team reaches the geographic North Pole.

Acknowledgments

It is hard to know where to start the overwhelming list of people we need to thank both for the completion of the book as well as the expedition it recounts. We are all humbled by the generosity of time, energy, commitment—and sometimes funding—we have received from others who believed in our project, in our message, and in us. We really do feel as if we have been on a journey with far more than just the sixteen who were on the ice.

Eugene Kaspersky, both personally and through his company Kaspersky Lab, has been our most instrumental supporter. Additional thanks to the Kaspersky Lab UK team, particularly Povel Torudd and Ruth Knowles, who didn't hesitate to help in any way they could.

We treasure the relationship with our sponsors and would like to thank Engie, OmanTel, Poseidon Expeditions, Kočevsko, I Feel Slovenia, La Communauté de Communes du Thouarsais, Lingling Wu, Sports Corner (Qatar), Honda al Ghanim (Kuwait), and General Sports Authority (Saudi Arabia) for their support of individual team members and the expedition. We were also provided with vital specialist expedition supplies, services, and equipment by BRBL, MultiMat, Tribe, Repharm, BLOC Eyewear, Montane, ColdAvenger, Buffera, iPadio, Nescafé, L'Occitane en Provence, Reebok, Panda supermarkets, Hilleberg the

249

tentmaker, and, in Reykjavik, Everest ehf. Summit to Eat provided us with beautiful freeze-dried meals including breakfast, freeze-dried fruits to make our snack bags during the day more interesting—and even desserts! The Institut polaire français Paul-Émile Victor kindly loaned us a submersion suit that we thankfully never needed to use but had a lot of fun trying—and failing—to put on in practice. Special thanks once again to Paul Cosgrove, this time at Berghaus, who supplied us with high-performance clothing. And to Carolyn Harker from Berghaus, who traveled to Longyearbyen to ensure the clothing was perfect and did us the honor of listening enthusiastically to our feedback on women's outdoor apparel in general.

In Oman we received valuable help from the fabulous Outward Bound Oman, headed by Mark Evans, and advice from Khalid al Wahaibi. During our time in Iceland we were grateful to Christof Girtsch, who not only wrote a marvelous article about us but also allowed himself to get far closer to the story than planned when he agreed to be roped in last minute to drive a minibus through a blizzard for us! Also the totally kick-ass Brynja Ejólfsdóttir for driving the truck and to Bjössi, Snorri, and Jökull, who came out in their enormous vehicles to collect us from the wilderness. (We will all remember for a very long time the moment the convoy of huge trucks pulled up beside the team as we skied in single file through the dark. "It's like a scene from a Hollywood movie!" exclaimed one excited teammate as we rapidly flung our sledges onto the trucks and roared off toward civilization at long last!) Our team-training expeditions in Iceland would not have happened if not for the generous support of our crowdfunding campaign by Simon Dannatt, Mazen abd Rabbo, Auditoire Qatar, Rachel Pearson, Joan O'Neill, David Dunn, Anke Wodarg, Whalley Warm & Dry, Steph Kiltie, Jean Sinclair, Libby Ruffle, Jessica, Kerstin Loehmann, Miriam Mozgan, Leva Lauraityte, Dalibor Cerar, Corrin Walters, Marycruz Olvera Esquivel, Ankit Chopra, Louisa Konaris, and Emily Chapman—you are our very special expedition angels.

Our expedition was enriched by the addition of a science program—thank you to Audrey Bergouignan and her team, who not only devised a brilliant science project but also came out to Longyearbyen and put impressive care and attention into making the project as straightforward as possible for us. We are indebted to the hospital in Longyearbyen and its very obliging staff for hosting and facilitating the science study before and after the expedition. Thanks also to Nathan Smith, who allowed us to take part in his fascinating research.

Exposure is the title of a feature-length film of our expedition created by the indefatigable Holly Morris. She and her team became part of the fabric of the expedition, and we greatly enjoyed spending time with Holly and producer Eleanor Wilson, as well as the two superwomen who were the camera operators on the ice, Kathryn Barrows and Ingeborg Jakobsen. Thanks also to polar legends Ann Daniels and Caroline Hamilton for taking on such a complicated project and for looking after the film team so well.

Every member of the expedition team really wants to thank the crew behind the operations at Barneo, not just for all their hard work on the ice but the many months of administration and organization behind the scenes beforehand. Leo Plenkin, thank you for all your patience and good faith, and to the two Victors (Victor Serov and Victor Boyarsky), thank you for all the encouragement and touching care you showed for the team that went above and beyond. Particular thanks for looking after Mariam so well when she needed it—and for deciding "No chop"!

Honored thanks to the two inspiring women who agreed to be our expedition patrons, Ségolène Royal and Violeta Bulc (EU commissioner for transport at the time). We are similarly grateful to Lindsay Wilson, who acted as our home support while we were on the ice; to Poonam Taneja from the BBC, who spent time with us in Longyearbyen to make a short film for BBC World that got our message to a vast audience; and to Rob Langford at Kaspersky Lab UK PR, who helped us with media interest—thank you all.

We were a flag-carrier expedition for WINGS World Quest, a fabulous organization supporting women in science and exploration and of which I am proud to be a fellow—thank you for your continued support. The Winston Churchill Memorial Trust (WCMT) supported our UK team member, Misba Khan, by awarding her a 2018 Churchill Fellowship. Having been appointed a Churchill Fellow myself in 2008, it was a unique moment for Misba and me to stand together at the North Pole flying the WCMT flag—an organization that continues to do so much to enrich UK society.

Creating a book from our collective experiences as a team was a very long road. I am thankful to Lee Constantine and Ben Nash at Publishizer for enabling a very innovative way to secure a publisher. I cannot thank enough Kevin Stevens at Imagine! Publishing, a Charlesbridge imprint, for not only securing the book but also for the months of hard work that followed in editing a vast number of words from several authors into a single unified narrative. A book written by a team together was an impossible idea, and yet we have made it work. Thanks for your advice, patience, and indulgence in letting us run with our ideas.

Equally important are the crowdfunders who preordered a copy of the book and have waited patiently for its delivery: Alan Grummitt, Alan Parkinson, Alen Bastia, Andy Lyon, Andy Leskowitz, Anna Gladkaya, Anne Brown, Ayuka Kawakami, Becci Jewell, Camilla White, Carole Williams, Cat Brandwood, Celina Laframboise, Claire Garnier, Claire Vivian, Claudia Schulz, Craig Carter, Cristina Fernandez, Dan Fox, Daniel Bratton, Daniela Helienek, Daphne Solomonidou, Ekaterina Veselina, Elena Neophytou, Elena Silaeva, Emma Khan, Evangelos Galiatsatos, Garrett Schnathorst, Hakam Kanafani, Hannah I'Anson, Helve Malmsaar, Holly Morris, Hugh Maguire, Iain McWilliam, Ian Berry, Igor Karnicnik, Ingeborg Jakobsen, Jamie Deas, Jasmina Kull, Jeanette James, Jennifer Murray, Jenny Dean, Jill Griebenow, Joan O'Neill, Joanne Scott, Jonny Went, Karen Zieff, Karen Oliveira Spofford, Katherine Watson,

Kelly Lewis, Kylie Stella, Lauren Rucigaj, Leslie Batten, Licet Sanchez, Lynne Arlow, Maggie Downham, Maike Chan, Maria Jonsson, Maria Luisa, Gonzalez Garcia, Marin Medak, Marinka de Wall, Marjana Lavric Sulman, Mark Wood, Mats Jonsson, Matthew Reed, Matthew Morgan, Mervyn Sims, Michael Pierides, Morven McLean, Nicholas Holden, Nicky Chisholm, Nigel Winser, Osamah Nijem, Patrick Peters, Paula Hazell, Pernille Sporon Boving, Peter McWilliam, Philip Green, Renee Muro, Rene Olsen, Richard Matthews, Rick Simms, Roger Makhlouf, Rohan Basu, Rok Sobiech, Sandi Rhys-Jones, Sandra Rutherford, Sarah McWilliam, Sarah Li-Hare, Sergey Ivanov, Shadi Ganjavian-Connor, Shannon Guzzo, Sharon Hope-Inglis, Shikhar Tiwari, Snjez Plevko, Soraya Abdel-Hadi, Stan Intihar, Steve Napier, Sue Fontannaz, Susan Sachs, Þorsteinn Viglundsson, Victor Matyushenkov, Vladimir Doronin, Alexandr Konovalov, Igor Cherkashin, Mikhail Yarin, and Ekaterina Rumyantseva. I very much look forward to sending you your very special copies with our thanks. We hope you feel as proud of it as we do.

Finally, my own biggest debt of gratitude is to my team members, who had the courage to step up and who trusted me to see them through. You were amazing and I learnt so much from you all. I look forward to reminiscing together about the wonderful memories we share for many more years. I'd also like to thank the families, friends, and employers who provided team members with the support and encouragement they needed in order to triumph at the top of the world. For my part, I need to say a very special thank-you to my husband, Gísli, and our little boy Þráinn Freyr (who was only eight months old at the time of the expedition) for being with me in Longyearbyen while I worked through all the stress of those final preparations and for sending me off on expedition with so much love. No matter where I go or what I do, you remain my favorite adventure of all.

Nataša thanks: I am extremely grateful to my main sponsors, Kočevsko and I Feel Slovenia, for recognizing the potential of our expedition and their generous help, and to BRBL, who really made it bearable. My special thanks go also to Polycom and Alpina. In preparation for this expedition I had the great pleasure of working with Olympic medalist Sara Isaković, a superwoman and first and foremost a wonderful person, who equipped me with much-needed mental skills and tools that allowed me to perform optimally in extremely cold weather conditions. I also had a great time working with fitness coach Simon Škoda. Thank you! To my friends and family, laughing in disbelief when they heard the news, knowing me and my fear of cold too well but supporting me all along. And to my friend Miriam, who was my biggest help and supporter from the start until I landed at Ljubljana Airport, where she organized a big welcome party at the airport. Thank you! And I would also like to thank everyone who followed our expedition through social media and sent kind messages, wishing us good luck! It meant a whole lot! Last but not least, Marin Medak, if it weren't for your tweet, I would have never heard of an expedition that gave me so much. Forever thank you!

Mariam thanks: I want to thank my parents, Amani and Alabbas, and my grandmother, Safia, for always supporting my choices even when they often defied the norm. To my brothers, Ibraheem, Ismael, and Yousef, and my sister, Nour, for cheering me every step of the way. Thank you to my best friend and chosen family, Samar, for always being there. Thank you to my husband, Usama, who was the last person I saw before getting on the plane for this journey and the first person I saw when I landed back home. I love you all. I am thankful to the people who made it so easy to ask for help—Mr. Hosam al Qurashi from Panda supermarkets for feeding the entire team, and the Saudi General Sports Authority for sponsoring me to go on this life-changing adventure. And to Bakeel Yamani, Yasmeen Gahtani, and Ahmed Sendi for immediately reaching out and offering their winter sports gear when I put up a post online asking for help. Thanks to all the amazing humans who passed through Barneo and shared their stories. They made my unexpectedly long stay at Barneo become one of the highlights of my trip. Special thanks to my doctor, Steinslav Boyarsky; the "hotel manager," Pavlik; and Barneo godfather Victor Serov. I want to thank my entire Euro-Arabian team for being strong, smart, kind, and real. I couldn't have chosen a better bunch of women, of sisters, to share this journey with. Finally, thank you to Felicity for bringing her vision to life against all odds and allowing us to share our story. I am grateful to have been a part of this.

Susan thanks: Merci à la Communauté de Commune du Thouarsais. I was lucky to have my hometown as my main sponsor for this extraordinary adventure. Not only the hometown but the *Thouarsais* and *Thouarsaises* who live there, kids and adults, friends and family, who followed me, who believed in me. Thanks to all the kids from the primary school of Luche Thouarsais and their enthusiastic teachers for sharing this adventure with me. I dedicate my story in this book to all those smiley little dreamers. Thank you to Norbert Bonneau for getting my hometown on board, and thank you to Annie Bonneau for helping me when visiting schools and colleges and doing radio interviews. Thanks to Emma, Johanne, and Elisa, my three wonderful nieces who made me realize that I had to share my adventure with kids. I also need to apologize to Elisa as I couldn't bring her back a piece of the North Pole. Most of my adventures involve my great friend Audrey Bergouignan, and this one is no exception as she was sitting next to me when I heard about the expedition. My friend Julie Gerecht was my "believe-in-yourself" coach when I prepared anxiously for my interview with Felicity. And there are so many more friends and family that were there along the way, in France, in Scotland, and the rest of the world. I can only say that you were with me on the Arctic ice. It was your love and friendship that warmed me when I was exhausted. Thank you to Pierre, Simon, and Alison for keeping up with their wandering sister. A big hug to my grandmother for providing me with the essential apron for my cooking duties during the expedition. Thank you, Mum—I wouldn't be where I am today without your love and support and giving me the confidence to follow my dreams. Thank you, Felicity, for making my North Pole dream come true, for allowing me to become a polar explorer and to share this adventure with so many. Thanks to all the team members of the Women's Euro-Arabian North Pole Expedition for sharing laughter and tears throughout the adventure and for providing me with some of the most exciting memories of my life. Finally, I would like to thank Iain for everything, but most of all for making me happy every day and for sharing our most beautiful adventure, our little Romy.

Lamees thanks: I would like to thank my family for their endless support throughout this journey and any journey I embark on in life. My father always taught me to own my decisions; he is a great believer in independence and gender equality. I would also like to thank my mother. She taught me to never let go of an opportunity and to see as much as I can of the world. I would also like to thank my older brothers, Hussein and Basel, for their endless support. They have always cheered for me, had my back. My twin sister, Liale, kept me going the entire journey. Whenever I'm in doubt, or have a moment of weakness, I run back to her. I would like to thank my sponsors for believing in me and believing in the cause behind this incredible expedition. Honda al Ghanim supported me throughout the training but also managed to create multiple media campaigns on the day we left for the North Pole and the day we reached it. I would also like to thank Elevation Burger for sending me all the way to Longyearbyen. And finally I would like to thank my dear friend Shahed Madi for connecting me with L'Occitane en Provence, who provided us with the best hand cream to use. And finally I would like to thank my friend Sara Tohmaz for arranging all the media coverage on radio and television on my way back to Kuwait. Special thanks to the Women's Euro-Arabian North Pole Expedition for every memory we had together, and a dearest thank-you to Felicity for making this all a reality.

Olga thanks: Thanks to my mom and my daughters, who are always waiting for me when I return from traveling.

Ida thanks: I would like to thank Nikolai Saveliev, president of Poseidon Expeditions, without whom I would not have been able to be part of this extraordinary adventure. Thank you, Jan Bryde, for helping me into the world of expedition ships in the Arctic and Antarctic, where I met this amazing woman, Felicity Aston, who inspired me so much. Thank you, Felicity, for making our dreams come true. You are not just an amazing teammate but a great friend. Thank you, Viking family, for all the support too—you have gone above and beyond to make us all succeed! I also want to thank my parents, Siw and Björn, for making me love the outdoors and always supporting me in all challenges I take on. You are always there for me and you are always in my heart. Thanks to my sister, Maria, for all the great adventures we have shared, which led to this lifetime of adventure. Thanks to my friends, who are always cheering me on. To Ryan, who encourages me and joins me on so many crazy adventures, thank you for all the love. Last but not least a big thanks to all my teammates—I am so proud of these women and so happy to have been part of such a wonderful team. Thank you all; keep living adventures and following your dreams!

Misba thanks: I would like to thank God Almighty for giving me the opportunity and guidance to achieve my goal and to be successful. I would like to thank my family, who have supported me throughout the journey; my friends, who have supported me with encouraging messages via social media; Manchester Coach Ramblers, who introduced me to the outdoors; Cotswold Outdoors Manchester, for helping me with equipment; and the Winston Churchill Memorial Trust for believing in me by awarding me a 2018 Churchill Fellowship. Felicity, thank you for making me part of an amazing group of women. Finally, if it wasn't for Jessica Hepburn I wouldn't have known about the expedition at all— thank you!

Steph thanks: First and foremost, a *huge* thank-you to Felicity for changing my trajectory in life and for taking me on an incredible ride of travel experiences in the past decade. You are truly an inspirational leader and teammate, and I am privileged to call you my friend. We have been so fortunate to have Eugene Kaspersky and his company Kaspersky Lab on board this expedition. I am very grateful for his support and have enjoyed meeting members of his amazing team over the years. My participation on the expedition would have been difficult without the generous support of Lingling Wu. Thank you for choosing our cause and our expedition to celebrate your landmark birthday! I would like to thank Adrian Stammers at Beacon Products for supporting our expedition—without our MultiMats I guarantee none of us would have gotten any sleep. Additionally, thank you to John Sullivan and the wonderful team at Talus for their messages of encouragement and our ColdAvenger Expedition balaclavas. As with the South Pole expedition in 2009, I have been fortunate with great media contacts and coverage, and this expedition was no exception. Thank you to Rosie Charalambous, Alix Norman, and Kyproulla Papachristodoulou. Finally, a massive thank-you to my parents, Roger and Soleil, for their unwavering support and for always having my back. To Matt, my driver/logistics manager/all-round awesome person, thank you for everything. Everyone needs cheerleaders in their life, and I am extremely blessed for all the enthusiastic encouragement from Cyprus, the UK, and around the world (the list is very long). Thank you friends, family, and work colleagues—you know who you are.

About the Author

Felicity Aston MBE is a British polar explorer and research scientist who has been creating and leading record-setting expeditions in the Arctic and Antarctic for more than twenty years. In 2012 she became the first woman to ski across Antarctica alone. In 2015 she was awarded the Queen Elizabeth II Polar Medal for services in the Arctic and Antarctic. Felicity has also been elected Fellow of the Royal Geographical Society (with the Institute of British Geographers) in London and is a Fellow of the Explorers Club in New York.